Cocaine

From Dependency to Recovery

2nd Edition

Cardwell C. Nuckols

Human Services Institute

SECOND EDITION
SECOND PRINTING

Library of Congress in Publication Data

Nuckols, Cardwell C.
Cocaine : from dependency to recovery / by Cardwell C. Nuckols. — 2nd ed.
p. cm.
Includes bibliographical references.
ISBN 0-8306-9203-7 (pbk.)
1. Cocaine habit. 2. Cocaine habit—Treatment. I. title.
RC568.C6N83 1989
616.86′47—dc20 89-5172
CIP

TAB BOOKS Inc. offers software for sale. For information and a catalog, please contact TAB Software Department, Blue Ridge Summit, PA 17294-0850.

Questions regarding the content of this book should be addressed to:

Human Services Institute, Inc.
P.O. Box 14610
Bradenton, FL 34280

Development Editor: Lee Marvin Joiner, Ph.D.
Copy Editor: Pat Holliday

Cover photograph by Susan Riley, Harrisonburg, Virginia.

Contents

Dedication

For all you've done and continue to do for the suffering alcoholic and addict . . .

Jokichi Takamine, M.D. and Hunter Copeland

Foreword

When a drug hits the market, there suddenly appears a rash of prophets, prognosticators, and pundits. Coupled with this fact are three traits of the American character:

> *We want things now;*
> *We like simple answers; and*
> *As a people who are basically pragmatic, if it works, use it; if it doesn't, get rid of it.*

Translated into language used in the field of sensory experience: if it gives pleasure, it is good; if it gives pain, it is bad.

Over the last few years, cocaine has assumed an ever increasing place in the center of the chemical dependency field, as well as in American culture. There has been a virtual outpouring of articles, books, and films either extolling its virtues or warning of its devastating and destructive nature.

In the campaign of 1986, Congress found "religion" in talking about drugs–particularly about cocaine and/or crack. I think it would be fair to say that there was a media hype which almost bordered on hysteria.

Cardwell Nuckols has written a book which, in my opinion, brings a well-needed measure of sanity and a rational perspective to this issue. It does not purport to be the definitive answer for, at this time in our history, there is no definitive answer or conclusion to the cocaine story. Combining a mixture of his own experience, and the shared experiences of countless others, all seasoned with a solid knowledge of the issue (theoretical and applied), this book offers to both lay people and professionals, a challenge, a learning opportunity, and a true sense of hope. If read carefully, the individual will get a much clearer understanding of this oftentimes deadly universal problem. In truth, no one can say that it is NOT my problem, for everyone in this country is at risk from any individual who uses drugs, cocaine being just one of the many available to our citizenry today.

Mr. Nuckols is to be thanked for bringing such a clear, coherent exposition of this insidious and frightening issue to the attention of the people of this country. As a doctor who has been working in the alcohol/drug abuse field for almost twenty-five years, I strongly recommend this book and thank Cardwell deeply for the privilege and the pleasure of having been allowed to write this brief foreword.

Jokichi Takamine, M.D.
Immediate Past Chairman,
AMA Task Force on Alcoholism

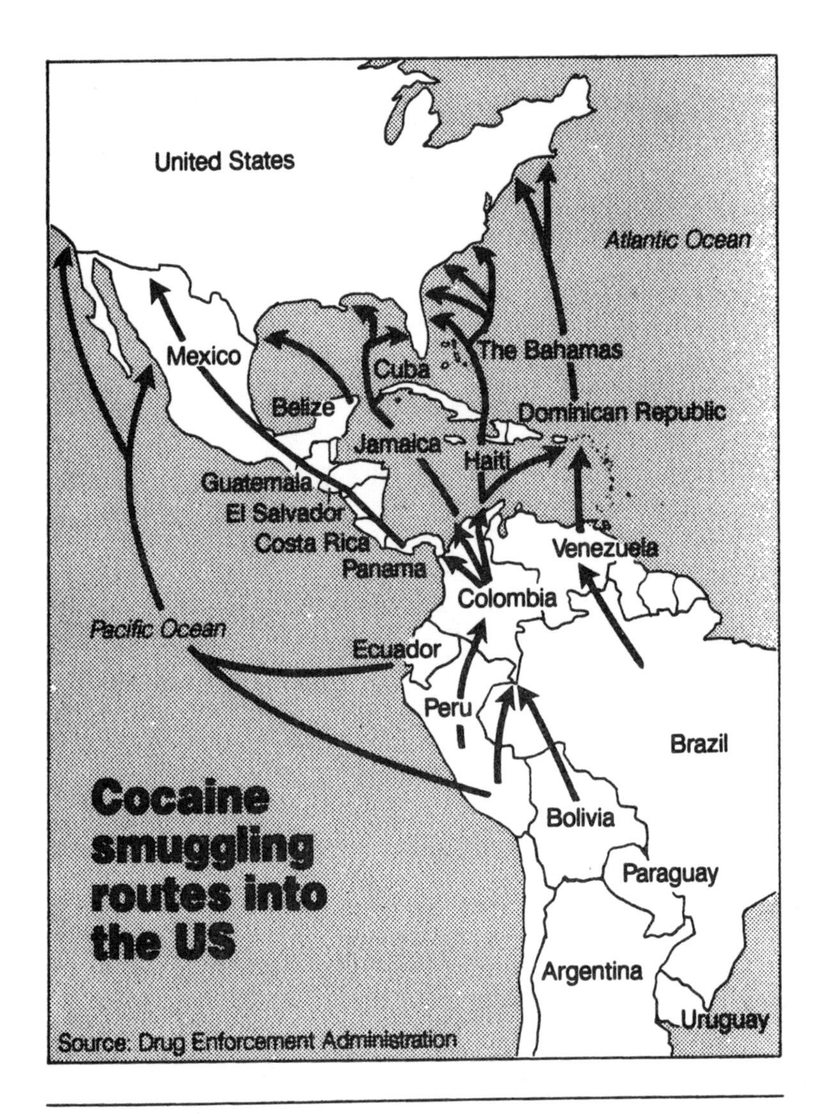

Remillard in The Christian Science Monitor © 1987 TCSPS

Preface

COCAINE: From Dependency to Recovery is a book for anyone concerned with cocaine dependence. Therapists, counselors, physicians, nurses, concerned family members and people who think they have developed a cocaine dependency problem can find useful information here. The material in the book arises from my own research and experience, first as a cocaine dependent and later as a therapist engaged in the treatment of cocaine addiction. I have tried to provide information and insights that I believe will help other therapists, cocaine addicts and their families, and concerned laymen to confront this serious human problem.

Some of the material in this book describes how therapists work with cocaine dependency. However, I must remind readers that experience, training, and supervision are crucial requisites for success as a therapist. No single book can provide all the answers, much less the experience. There is often a mystique surrounding the therapy process and a tendency to consider techniques "secret."

However, therapy is an interaction between therapist and patient, directed in this instance toward the goal of recovering from an addiction. The more both participants in the process know about each other–their motives, assumptions, and objectives–the better the chance of recovery. Families of cocaine addicts should know everything they can about the treatment process in order to support, rather than obstruct, it. There should not be any secrets.

An aura of glamour and mystery surrounds cocaine. The mystique is heightened by special terms and concepts that create social distance between cocaine users and those not involved in "the cocaine culture." First, we should be aware that cocaine wasn't always considered "evil." There are classic stories conveying a positive image of cocaine use. For example, the man who designed the Statue of Liberty wrote a letter to a gentleman who produced a wine preparation laced with cocaine:

My dear Mr. Mariani:

If I had only had your magic elixir when I was designing the Statue of Liberty, the statue would have been at least 100 meters taller.

Consider Sigmund Freud and the glamour ascribed to his use of cocaine in psychiatric treatment. Freud treated many ailments with cocaine: dyspepsia, alcoholism, narcotics addiction, and depression. He sent it to his lover to relieve her depression.

Robert Lewis Stevensen was treated with cocaine for tuberculosis. During his treatment he wrote Dr. Jekyl and Mr. Hyde. It is said that he wrote it in three days. Ironically, cocaine has become the Dr. Jekyl and Mr. Hyde of all drugs. No other substance I know has the propensity to cause the problems which this drug can cause.

There is much material available to readers on the bare facts about cocaine and the horror stories surrounding its use. It is relatively easy to learn about the pharmacology of the drug. Nevertheless, as some addicts cling to the power legends of cocaine, many "outsiders" including professional therapists and counselors, remain intimidated by the language and culture of cocaine addiction. For instance, anyone "have a summer cold?" Ever "eaten a doughnut in the bathroom" and gotten the white powder on your nose? Have you "Captain Kirked," "gone to see Scottie," "beamed up," or been a "rock star?" Semantic barriers like these must be overcome if you, as a family member, friend, or therapist, want to understand and help the cocaine addict.

What is the cocaine addict like? People who have never been dependent on cocaine have no clear idea of its effects. If you are an alcohol counselor and recovering yourself, or if you have had trouble with marijuana, Valium, or Librium, you can relate to the experiences of people with similar drug dependency problems. If you are an alcoholic or have ever been drunk and hung over, you can sit down and know how a client feels. You can get right into their system and experience. But when a cocaine addict says, "I went out and copped an eight-ball last night," or "I went out basing and balling," you may say, "What was this person doing?" What is the cocaine addict's reality? Many people, often therapists and counselors, who would like to help, are intimidated by the language of cocaine.

Without the language and the shared experiences, you may look at the cocaine user in an entirely different light. He or she may offend and repel you. You can't penetrate their reality. Beyond this, the addict may begin to convey a sense of uniqueness or specialness. Attitudes, words and actions are chosen to convey, "I am special."

Cocaine addicts want to be special. They seek power and control. When you try to establish communication and rapport there will be a test. If you don't know an "eight-ball" is an eighth of an ounce of cocaine (or 3.5 grams), if you don't know what "freebasing" is, don't know how to "fire up" cocaine, and don't understand colloquialisms such as "speed-balling" (cocaine laced with heroin), you will have difficulties.

Cocaine addicts don't perceive themselves as addicts. They see themselves as productive people. They don't like inpatient remedies. They like outpatient solutions. And they often want to talk about physical problems. It doesn't make any difference what type of person you're dealing with. It doesn't make any difference if they freebase cocaine or use it intravenously. The difference is in how we deal with them. Much of the content of COCAINE describes methods I have used to help cocaine addicts recover. In this book I try to portray a realistic picture of cocaine: the experience, the drug, the addiction, and the hard realities of recovery.

One thing I stress is that counselors bear fifty percent of the responsibility for creating the motivation for the cocaine addict's recovery. I often hear counselors say, "Gee, I guess this person just needed a little more field research; they needed to go and fall on their face once or twice more." As a former director of several chemical dependency programs, it breaks my heart to hear this. When cocaine addicts insist on outpatient remedies, want to focus discussion on physical problems, and are unwilling to work hard with you to enter an inpatient environment,

I think it is time to start planting some seeds. Help create the motivation for recovery.

I think of the case of a man who attended a community seminar in Miami. He was in the back row and would get up and walk out every fifteen minutes. I assumed he was going to the bathroom, "eating some doughnuts," or something. I talked to him later and it was interesting. People who use cocaine put on a face, but they are basically lonely and desperate, with many problems. This man came up to me and said, "C.C., I like what you said. You talked about me today. I can see myself in all of what you've talked about. I've had a seizure, sinus problems, and upper respiratory tract infections for over four years now. I smuggle cocaine . . . just brought ten pounds of freebase in from the Bahamas." This man continued, "Look, I don't want to talk about going into treatment; I don't want to talk about problems. All I want to know is: what will happen to me next, physically? And I want someone to talk to because, you see, it's lonely here."

An agony was inside this man, but cocaine's grandiosity and the strange things it did to his mind were all there too. I talked to him for a little while. He came from an upper middle-class family, a lawyer's son, and had been through college. He had a career and was in the process of "blowing" it all. He reminded me of another person I worked with who was a vice-president of a corporation. The first time I met him his family came to me for an intervention. He lived in a luxurious home. In nine months, he was selling cocaine on the street, living in the worst part of Chicago. When you walked into his house, there was human excrement on the floor. Cocaine is a powerful drug! People can't stop . . . without help.

Chapter 1

THE COCAINE EXPERIENCE

A well-known comedian I'll call Bill, recounts this conversation with a cocaine addict. He said, "Now why do you use that stuff? Can't you see that it's screwing up your life?" The person turned to him and said, "But Bill, you know it intensifies your personality." Bill looks at him and says, "Yeah, but what if you're a jerk?"

Many people find cocaine a pleasant experience as long as they are around the people, places and things that reinforce the use of the drug, and no adulterants are in the drug to cause difficulty. A lot of people like to go to bars and use cocaine; others like to sit around the house and use it. Under these conditions cocaine produces intense pleasure sensations.

Among cocaine's nicer qualities is that it causes euphoria and general stimulation. In looking at the direct pharmacological effects of cocaine, you see that it shares attributes of the sexual act itself. When a person starts to become excited, what does cocaine do? On a biochemical level, it intensifies.

Cocaine does some profound things to the brain. In producing the perception of euphoria, it acts directly on the reward center of the brain. In 1954 James Olds investigated this center. He took electrodes and stimulated various areas of monkeys' brains. When precise areas of the brain were electrically stimulated, the monkey would get an erection or ejaculate without the presence of a female. All drugs that alter consciousness appear to act on this same part of the brain.

When you have a chemical that's behaviorally reinforcing because of its pleasurable action on the brain, what are the odds of using it again? There is nothing that gives a quicker emotional "turnaround" than cocaine. A pattern of repeated use arises when past behavioral reinforcement tells the brain there is no quicker way to feel good than to use cocaine.

Cocaine itself is an anesthetic, but it's a rare drug because it is also sympathomimetic. It mimics the effect of the sympathetic nervous system. The sympathetic nervous system is what triggers feelings of anxiousness and the fight-or-flight reaction for self-preservation. Have you ever been frightened? If you can, recall how you felt then. Fear is biochemically similar to someone "getting off" on cocaine.

There are parallels between the effects of cocaine and of alcohol withdrawal. In a withdrawing alcoholic you see increased heart rate, enlarged pupils, increased blood pressure and psychomotor agitation. They are "all over the place." If you've ever watched the effects of withdrawal from alcohol, you have a good idea of the direct effects of cocaine intoxication.

Cravings, both for cocaine itself and for the heightened excitement surrounding its use, are a major aspect of the cocaine experience. These cravings for excitement often produce the biggest problems in treating the addiction itself. I use this story with clients to illustrate how the excitement and risk-taking dimension is involved in the addictive pattern. The clients' reactions to the story help me anticipate with whom I'm going to have the most problems, in terms of craving for excitement.

I say, "You know, there are two types of cocaine people whom I run into. I'm just going to ask you to identify which one you're most like. Which one represents you?" I go on to say, "You know, there's one kind of cocaine addict who drives down a road he's never been down before, an old, winding, mountain road, driving sixty miles an hour, screaming around the curves. In the middle of the night, all of a sudden, the headlights flash upon a big 'Bridge Out' sign. He slams on the brakes; comes sliding to a screeching halt; gets out and looks around; and finds he is only one foot away from going over a 200-foot embankment into a river. He looks at it and says, 'Oh, my God, I almost died.'"

"There's a second type of cocaine addict who starts screaming down that same road, never having been there before in his life. He's going sixty or seventy miles an hour around a curve, and then his lights flash on a sign that says, 'Road Closed. Bridge Out.' He slams on the brakes, comes sliding in, a foot short of going over, looks down and says, 'Hum, one foot short; not bad, huh?'"

The second type of individual is going to have a lot of problems with cocaine addiction. They're the type of people who like the thrill; they like to test their program. They're the type of people who are like the alcoholic we used to watch go back into the bar and try to have a ginger ale with the fellows. They think nothing is any good unless they test it, push it to the edge. It's only at the extreme edge of experience that something becomes important.

Sometimes when I tell cocaine addicts that story, and I begin the second part, you know which one they're going to choose because they start to beam and glow and float away while you're telling them the story. They can see themselves there saying, "Yeah, I bet I could have been six inches closer."

Cocaine as Lover

The feeling of the adrenalin rush of cocaine is like the feeling of falling in love. We have to understand that basic feeling in order to really appreciate the magnetic pull of the cocaine experience. Again and again we see that a relationship has evolved between the user and the drug cocaine, often an intense primary relationship which overshadows all others.

This has always seemed quite remarkable to me. Last year we produced some videos for treatment programs. To illustrate my point, I remember one particular scene in the video where a lady said, "Gees, my husbands (in plural) said to me, 'It's either the cocaine or me.'" Her response universally was, "There's the door; get the hell out." This profile is less often encountered in addiction to other substances.

When clients describe their involvement with cocaine, it often seems as though they are telling the story of an intense love affair.

> *"My cocaine use started out one, two years ago. In the beginning I only did it at a party. I only did it when someone turned me on. Then I started to buy it. I started to buy it and sell a little bit of it, so I'm*

getting into different behaviors with different groups of people. And then, I got into episodes where I lost control of my use; it was no longer situational and I was getting a bunch of cocaine that I wanted to sell and my plans were that I was going to get it on Thursday night and I was going to have a gram for Friday, and I was going to have a little bit for the party Saturday, but by Friday morning I had done it all. That was my first loss of control; the first time we watched the sun come up."

A few writers have tried to capture the feeling and mood of cocaine-as-lover. In the book *Bright Lights; Big City* there is a romantic mood-piece which is a beautiful description of the pivotal junction between 2 and 6 in the morning, when you lose track of time, and suddenly find yourself standing on the corner of Walk and Don't Walk, a buzz on and no place to go.

But cocaine is a drug that can terrify you, make you seem alien to yourself, weird. If you do enough heroin, you don't give a damn; you can flop in the nicest hotel lobby in downtown Chicago–and I've seen it happen a few times–and you don't care. It's a permanent vacation–your brain is shut off. Not so with cocaine. The peculiar, estranged feeling about yourself which accompanies long-term use of cocaine is often magnified by its side effects and compounded by the use of alcohol and Valium, two drugs whose use frequently goes along with cocaine addiction.

As the cocaine relationship enters the marital state, the amount and frequency of its use rises sharply. And what we hear and see, over and over, is that the experience isn't social any more. Cocaine has become the jealously guarded and protected lover. Instead of being an overt, "Let's do a few toots in the bathroom," a little "Bolivian march encounter," what begins to happen is the secret hoarding of cocaine.

The cocaine user begins to have only a select group of one or two or three people with whom he uses. He goes "undercover" with the cocaine. At about the time the cocaine use becomes covert, he starts to use depressant drugs more frequently. The result is that, if you're among this user's family and friends, you will probably have no accurate picture of the amount of cocaine being used. Instead, you'll probably start to see an increasing use of alcohol as a depressant. For example, someone intoxicated on cocaine will, if he has to be around his family, often drink heavily to "mellow out," maybe smoke a few joints, do a few pills.

As a therapist, I've heard this story repeated many times in different words and dialects: "I can't understand my wife. She's drinking and smoking dope and staying up for two or three days. It doesn't make any sense." What has usually happened is that she has gone "undercover" with the cocaine, but the drugs that she wouldn't mind losing quite as much–the alcohol and other drugs–she is using very overtly.

The tendency to go "undercover" with the cocaine explains why we often need information from friends and family to obtain an accurate picture of the cocaine user's addictive pattern. It also explains why a therapist often must ask questions which might seem to have nothing to do with cocaine. For example, how many fifths of liquor are seen around the house? Is he often coming home intoxicated? What about prescription bottles? What about pot? How many joints do you see him smoke? From the standpoint of effective treatment, accurate information about the addict's drug use pattern is essential.

A Drug for the '90's

Cocaine addiction in America today has been described as an epidemic. Epidemiologists, the professionals who track and study epidemics, have concluded that anywhere from 5,000 new people a day to 5,000 a week experiment with cocaine. The total number of people in this country who have used cocaine is estimated-to-be from 20 to 25 million. This number is about half the number of Americans who have experimented with marijuana. Would a flower-child in the late '60's and early '70's have imagined any illegal substance would ever equal marijuana on the black market as the national drug-of-choice? Cocaine has started to do so.

The 1986 University of Michigan high school senior survey, which is a good source of information about future drug trends, found just about all the drugs being either stabilized or reduced in terms of percentage of the seniors who have experimented with them, with the exception of crack and cocaine, which continue to climb. Ten years ago, only about 8 percent of the high school seniors had even experimented once with cocaine. By 1985 that percentage had risen to 17.8 and it is still climbing.

Today in America we have a population of people using cocaine to self-medicate, using cocaine because it gives them feelings of power and control, and using it because it augments their hyperactive lifestyle. They like cocaine's euphoriant properties. Some people just feel they deserve cocaine because they work hard–they deserve to take $100 and go out and grind their teeth and become paranoid.

Why have we turned so excessively to cocaine now? It has been available for a long time, well over one hundred years. Typically, people have spent less time and energy trying to answer this question than attempting to stop people from using the drug. For example, the *1986 Drug Abuse Act* emphasized interdiction, preventing cocaine from entering the country. But as a therapist, I have observed that the "cocaine problem" is more a societal, than a supply, issue. As long as there is a demand, someone's going to find a way to meet it, to supply the drug. Right now, in spite of the interdiction effort, more and better quality cocaine is being imported at a lower price than ten years ago.

When you talk to people who use cocaine and listen to their self-reports, much of cocaine's appeal stems from its ability to produce euphoria. The energizing properties of the drug help overcome depression and dysphoria. It increases feelings of assertiveness, self-esteem, and tolerance for frustration. It eliminates feelings of boredom and emptiness. In addition, there is aggressive, and sometimes creative, marketing of the drug; cocaine is a business. For the adolescent/young adult population, with limited financial resources, the cocaine merchants have done exactly as the pharmaceutical companies did in the past; they've unit dosed. You can buy an inexpensive unit dose of crack or rock, but if you buy enough unit doses to make a gram, it represents about what you'd have to pay for cocaine hydrochloride, the type of cocaine you inject or snort. However, unit dosing increases the breadth of the potential consumer market and the accessibility of the drug.

I have concluded, however, that there is more to the appeal of cocaine than its ability to produce euphoria and its ever-broadening availability. I think it is no coincidence that when we started the breakdown of our families and the "do your own thing" movement, we began to see the emergence of a cocaine problem. Along with this came the compelling idea of entitlement. "I am entitled to freedom, stimulating experiences, and fulfillment." Cocaine magnifies this sense of entitlement. Exhibitionism–including sexual exhibitionism–flourishes when people are high on cocaine. And, as is true with any chemical dependency, you see a deepening level of interpersonal exploitation. Cocaine causes us to exploit others in meeting what we perceive to be our own personal needs.

I've been impressed over the years by why people "do" the drugs they do. I started to look at why people selected cocaine in the late 70's, early 80's as the drug of choice. When I started to look back I noted that the decade of the 1950's was an interesting time in our country–a prosperous stable time. The early 1960's were still pleasant; things were very good for us. We had alcohol problems and some prescription drug problems, but on the whole it was a good time for our country.

As we reached the late 1960's and early 1970's, something started to happen that I think is still affecting us today. That something is the "me generation." We started to hear people like Timothy Leary say, "Drop out, tune in, turn on." We started to see an era of narcissism, to an extreme we'd never seen before. If we look at what society values and what emerged in this era of narcissism, we find data that speak to the issues of why we look to cocaine for the peace we believe is missing inside us.

The Family Connection

Looking around the country at people who are having cocaine-related difficulties, both adolescents and adults, we see some revealing data. For example, I talked with a therapist, a psychologist from San Francisco, named Kathleen O'Connell. She said that in her private practice of twelve or thirteen years, ninety to ninety-five percent of all the cocaine addicts whom she's treated came from dysfunctional homes, primarily homes where there was alcoholism.

This is a true story and I think it speaks to the heart of this issue, the problem of family values. I once lived in Chicago's Oak Forest area and had an office in Lombard, Illinois, close to the rich northwest suburbs of Chicago. One Sunday when I was getting ready to leave town I received a call from a perplexed mother who said, "You've just got to meet with our son. We think that he has a cocaine problem." I agreed that on my way to the airport I would stop and spend an hour with them–Mom, Dad, and son.

Soon after I got there Mom and Dad drove up in their brand new Cadillac. We sat there and talked for about fifteen minutes, waiting for Junior to show up. A very interesting thing happened: their son showed up in a $30,000 Porsche. I looked at Mom and Dad and said, "Did you buy this car for your son?" And they said, "No." I said, "Well, how did he get the money . . . to purchase this automobile?" They looked at each other, and Mom looked at Dad, and Dad looked back at Mom, and they looked at each other again . . . and suddenly Mom turned to me and said, "Well, I guess he must have gotten a part-time job." This is a dysfunctional family! I have personally treated cocaine addiction for twelve years and have noticed the disproportionately large number of addicts coming from dysfunctional family backgrounds. Often, alcohol is involved.

Cocaine addicts describe backgrounds like my own, having said things like, "I'm never going to grow up to be like Dad." My own father was an alcoholic physician who died at age 49 of liver and kidney failure. And I was never going to grow up to be like him! So I grew up to be a cocaine addict.

Someone who comes from an addictive family background is comfortable with that lifestyle. In many ways that addictive lifestyle, the ups and downs, mimics the cocaine experience beautifully. How do you solve problems in a dysfunctional, addictive family? Crap hits the fan? Slap a band-aid on it. Go on a honeymoon. That's why a lot of alcoholic couples say, "Gees, we like to fight because we like making up. You know, that's when we make love–drink a bottle of champagne and make love. And when the tension rebuilds–crap hits the fan–we solve it by having a little fight, blowing off steam . . . having another bottle of champagne and sex !" That is a typical dynamic.

In an addictive family you don't learn to maintain stability, to solve the fundamental problems. In the addictive family you just learn that when it's bad enough and you're feeling bad enough, you take action; you do something. What you do may be to go out and get drunk, while your wife runs into the bedroom and cries. Now this is an exciting lifestyle. You never can be sure of the outcome of any given sequence of events. Ask children of alcoholics about Christmas, a nearly-universal, positive experience in America. What they will usually tell you is that some of them were extremely good and some of them were awful. You never really knew how it would turn out. It all depended on Dad and how much he drank–whether he got into a fight with Uncle Charlie. Everyone was on edge.

So you've grown up and out of this family and now you're addicted to an exciting, stimulating drug, a drug that in many ways simulates the American dream: it gives you energy; it keeps your weight down; it's an aphrodisiac according to some sources; it mimics the excitement of a personal, intimate connection.

Still, coming from a dysfunctional family, your self-esteem is probably poor. Perhaps you don't know exactly who you are. Maybe your ego is not exactly what you would like it to be. Maybe at times you don't feel that you belong. There may be a profound sense of isolation. A loaded question for you is, "Who are you and what do you want?" Remember these issues of ego, identity, self-esteem, and belonging as we consider the role of cultural conditioning.

Cocaine and Culture

Cocaine blends with the economics, politics, and social psychology of America in the 1980's like bathtub gin in the 1930's. Culturally conditioned aspirations, folk heroes and the hyperbole of advertising indirectly reinforce cocaine use, even as it is officially condemned. Judgments about personal worth stress achievements, not who you are. Are you a vice-president? Do you own your own company? How much money do you make?

To illustrate how our culture reinforces these values, consider the questions, "When was the last time someone asked you about your spiritual program? When was the last time someone asked you about how good a parent you are? How good a husband? How good a wife? When was the last time someone asked you what we should do to change things back to a more pleasant way of life, when the family was the focus–before we started to see the disruption of the family and the problems of separation and divorce we have today?"

For the masses, usually young, who lack the glitter and don't expect to achieve it, cocaine is seductive. I recall conversations with cocaine users like this: "If you live in a neighborhood where everyone has a Cadillac, you have to have at least a BMW or a Mercedes." A one-up social climate like this permeates the psychology and behavior of everyone. In a society that places so much emphasis on externals, on what you do and what you accomplish, a drug like cocaine creates a quick and dirty avenue for fulfilling human needs. Remember, "He who gets the most toys before he dies wins!"

Ironically, it isn't only the person who doesn't achieve according to cultural ideals who becomes involved with cocaine. I've counseled people who are cocaine dependent even though they are super-successes by our cultural standards. In male cocaine addicts we often see family heroes, people who judge themselves, and are judged, by what they do in the world of work. These people are out there hustling, but inside they feel empty. For these victims of their own success, cocaine fulfills a missing sense of importance and boosts feelings of self-worth. Preoccupied with the fantasy of unlimited success, power, brilliance, beauty or ideal love, they embrace cocaine. What is missing is internal peace, internal gratification, internal reward.

Take these two extremes, the external priorities of our society and the numbers of people with perceived internal deficits, and add something that brings these two realms together to make a whole. That something is cocaine. Cocaine is a drug that enhances one's sense of ego. It creates the illusion of belonging. It is a power and control drug for people who are hustling in the fast lane, but who, on the inside, still feel they don't belong. They feel that they're not everything in the world they want to be. When you add cocaine, suddenly there's a feeling of wholeness. Cocaine provides a sense of power, potency and control that they may not have felt before. This is the common denominator of the drug of choice of the 1980's.

To appreciate the appeal of cocaine to the adolescent or young adult exposed to today's social pressures, consider an advertisement for a cocaine treatment program. On one side of the brochure is a list of the properties of cocaine, and on the other side, a list of the problems it causes. You read the properties of cocaine and see that it makes you feel alert. It causes you to lose your appetite so it makes you slim and trim. People will love you because it causes you to talk a lot. ("I'm shy and have trouble going out and meeting people.") Besides all these things, cocaine causes you to feel euphoric. "I'm not going to read the other side of the brochure, because I know that this must be the drug for me."

If you think about this, in the 80's, these are the important things to have. We want to be trim. We want to be the life of the party. We want to be out there and be involved. Cocaine helps us meet these needs.

Feelings

What is a person's subjective experience when he snorts a couple of lines of cocaine? If you think about two people who sit down and snort cocaine and talk to one another, it's almost as if they met every criteria for the diagnosis: narcissistic personality disorder. They have an exaggerated sense of self-importance. The universe revolves around them. They adopt the posture of important people. If you have low self-esteem or if you're vulnerable to power and control urges, cocaine is the drug for you.

People with poor self-esteem, stressed and bored, have a high incidence of cocaine use. To augment a hyperactive, restless lifestyle and the need for self-sufficiency, people use cocaine. Like every drug I've known, whether a depressant or stimulant, cocaine gives the feeling that you're in control. Paradoxically, cocaine is a profound central nervous system stimulant. When someone uses it you'd think it would make them rattle a little. But most people describe an enhanced sense of internal control when using cocaine.

If you've been around addicts you've heard some of the things they talk about. One thing that's prominent is the association between sex and cocaine. Many people see cocaine as an aphrodisiac. At low doses the male can maintain an erection for hours. They aren't orgasmic.

However, if two regular sex partners are frequent cocaine users, the quality of their relationship is affected by the drug. There's emotional distancing in the relationship. Probably the only thing they're giving each other in the relationship is cocaine. They probably have poor communication and have never looked each other in the eye. Who would want to look at someone with cocaine eyes anyway? They aren't a pretty sight to see.

As cocaine use accelerates, males lose the ability to have an erection and the ability to have an orgasm. And you start to get kinky to compensate for your lost sexual performance. Some of the stories told by everyday middle class Americans using cocaine sound like scripts for X-rated movies. People who preferred "man on top, get it over quick" are now "into" sadomasochism and bondage. The behavioral alterations, the physiological and psychological changes produced by cocaine are profound.

Especially with males, sexual fantasy surrounds cocaine use and even recovery from it. Oral sex themes are prominent. For example, a strong threat to recovery exists for the client who is now in treatment but who was accustomed to exchanging cocaine for sexual favors. In his perception, his needs are no longer being met and he starts to do a lot of fantasizing. This makes it essential to minimize his exposure to pornographic material, to help him control fantasizing to some degree, so he doesn't start to get back into that old dynamic, the profound sexual allure of cocaine.

Although there is more information available about the sexual dimensions of men's cocaine addiction, women's special problems are becoming recognized. A relatively high incidence of incest can create serious sexual problems for female addicts.

When you try to generalize about the effects of cocaine, whether administered intravenously, intranasally, or smoked as freebase, you must consider several things beyond the drug itself. For example, if you are talking about total drug effect, there are many subpopulations of users. This is true for any substance of abuse. Some people experience intense anxiety from just one marijuana cigarette. Many things combine to create a drug's effect. A complex set of interactions influence one's response to cocaine: 1) the direct pharmacological effect of the drug; 2) the effects of cuts or adulterants added to the drug; 3) the personality of the user; 4) the physical and social environment; and, 5) alcohol and other drugs used in combination with the cocaine.

Among the most important sources of cocaine's effects are the internal and external cues associated with its use. Internal cues are represented by the psychological make-up of the individual user. Internal cues include the person's perception, past experience, expectations, and all the biochemical events occurring in the body. Internal cues include how a person feels today. Are you sick? Have you eaten well?

External cues are primarily what may be called the people, places and things. Things are money in the pocket, Eric Clapton's cocaine song on the radio, different sorts of cues associated with using cocaine.

What if someone told you he or she had done cocaine and turned into a raving monster? Your perception might be that if you take cocaine you will have a negative reaction. This beforehand perception of the event may cause you to have an unsatisfactory, distressing experience. In contrast, if someone told you, "Cocaine is the most marvelous drug you'll ever do in your life. Do a couple of lines of cocaine and you'll be in heaven," your perception of the drug's effect would be different.

Consider the setting for cocaine use. You are out in the world of people, places and things, and you are out "doing some cocaine." In contrast, let's suppose you are in a sterile, white laboratory where a technician is administering cocaine. Your experiences will be different. Probably the anxiety that cocaine can cause will be in the forefront. If you are in a situation where the external cue is a beautiful woman in a dimly lit setting, offering cocaine as a precursor to sexual intercourse, you will have a different drug experience than in the laboratory. Set and setting are important determinants of your drug experience.

Drug effects are often mediated by some of the cuts or adulterants that are used to extend or dilute the substance. If a cocaine user says he took one toot and went directly to the bathroom, what he is possibly telling you is that the cocaine was cut with a baby laxative called Monito. Monito is a cut that looks good. Its white crystalline flakes look just like the drug itself and it has little effect of its own.

What else is used as cut in street cocaine? What adulterants are used? At the time of this writing, street cocaine has become very potent, and is getting stronger. Cuts that are popular today are mannitol and inositol. Cocaine is also cut with lidocaine, procaine or any of the 'caines.' These are all anesthetics which give you that freeze that mimics the direct anesthetic effect of cocaine.

Some substances used to cut or adulterate cocaine can be highly dangerous or toxic. We're now beginning to find freebase or rock and crack which is cut, but the typical user has no way of knowing what is used as an adulterant. Nor do we know the exact techniques used. I haven't seen this directly, but have heard that Drano is one of the substances now being used as a cutting agent for crack.

There are other substances on the street that mimic the effect of cocaine. Have you ever read a head magazine, where you see mail order ads for white crystalline powders that you can stuff up your nose? It's not cocaine and not illegal. They're the "look-alikes." We've had the look-alike amphetamines, the little black biphetamine, "black beauty," sold somewhat legitimately through stores. Well, the same thing is happening with cocaine. There have been some studies showing that people who use cocaine can actually "get off" on the placebo effect.

Although cocaine is a powerful drug, the placebo effect can be taken advantage of. If you went out tonight and bought one hundred dollars worth of something that was junk, you'd "get off" on it. That is the placebo effect. You'll find it over and over again. Often, experienced users can't tell the difference between cocaine and lidocaine, perhaps a primary component of the gram they just bought.

Cocaine has some side effects that are discouraging. It causes you to grate your teeth and get all tight. You sometimes see almost a heroin-type syndrome when you have a person come into treatment saying his muscles hurt. You say to yourself, "That is not what cocaine withdrawal is supposed to look like." But that is what it looks like if you've been tight for two days. When you're all hunched over and tight, once those muscles start to relax, they get very tender and sore. Side effects are why high-dose users display a common pattern. The uncomfortable side effects of cocaine are edginess, anxiety, and paranoia. In reaction, high-dose users will begin using central nervous system depressants to "take the edge off," to take a little of the crank off the drug.

It's becoming common to see paranoid responses among high-dose cocaine users. They run to the window every time a car goes by to see if it is the police. Then they begin using other drugs to help titrate the dysphoric effects of the cocaine.

Unless a person has a genuine psychiatric problem, his cocaine paranoia will be an exaggeration of his immediate fears. If he's a street dealer he's likely to believe the narcs are in the closet. If he's been "ripping off" his company and works for the Chicago Board of Trade, he's going to be afraid the IRS is in the closet. This kind of paranoia is an exaggeration of a normal and understandable fear, magnified and continuous.

So the most common thing you'll notice in a behavioral profile of a cocaine addict is escalation. Besides more and more cocaine, they will be alcohol and pot. This is your typical profile. Often you'll see other central nervous system depressants used such as Quaaludes. You'll see Valium, Librium, and other tranquilizers and sleeping pills–any form of central nervous system depressant. Heroin and other opioids are also commonly utilized.

The cocaine experience, then, is a variety of individual reactions to the drug, based upon an even greater variety of internal and external factors. It is the result of societal and cultural values and pressures. A far-reaching, illegal, unregulated and highly profitable business responds to those values and pressures. This combination of individual users, of societal pressures and of enormous profits is the cocaine experience of the '80's. In Chapter 2, we'll examine the central element of this experience, cocaine, the drug itself.

Chapter 2

COCAINE: THE DRUG

Cocaine is an illegal drug, smuggled into the United States primarily from South America (see map page *vii*). The coca plant, whose leaves supply the drug, requires high altitudes to grow. Soil, altitude and climatic conditions in the Andes Mountains of South America are ideal for cocaine horticulture. Recently, however, we've begun to see some attempts at growing the coca plant in the United States. In 1985, coca plants were discovered growing on the Hawaiian Islands and arrests were made.

Cocaine is considered a "Schedule II" drug by the United States federal government. A Schedule II drug is one with high potential for abuse, but having legitimate medical uses. First offense penalties for trafficking in cocaine range from five to fifteen years in prison and a fifteen to twenty-five thousand dollar fine. Appendix B contains an overview of the *Controlled Substances Act of 1970* which governs federal drug penalties.

In the mountains of South America, cocaine was used by the Indians for generations. Native Indians worked long hours at high altitudes with little food. By chewing the coca leaves, as some Americans chew tobacco, their appetites were reduced. The absorption of the drug through the mucous membrane provided an energizing effect. Chewing the coca leaf made them feel more like working and less like eating. These attributes were important among people who worked long hours in the mountain air with low oxygen content. To them, coca leaves were a blessing, a gift from the Sun God.

Epidemic II

The use of cocaine in the United States today is quite a different story. Here, cocaine use has been called an epidemic. One of the characteristics of an epidemic is that it is a temporary prevalence of a particular disease. In an epidemic, a disease appears suddenly, spreads rapidly and affects large numbers of people. Eventually, the epidemic abates. A well-known epidemic, which resulted in more deaths–in a brief period of two years–than any war in American history was the influenza epidemic of 1918-1920. As suddenly and inexplicably as it began, it stopped. We cannot be sure whether or not this abatement will occur in the case of today's cocaine upsurge, but it may be worthwhile to consider what happened in an earlier epidemic of cocaine addiction which impacted the United States between 1885 and 1920. In preparing an effective strategy for dealing with cocaine addiction on a national scale, or even locally, we must make projections about the future.

During the first ten years of our earlier cocaine epidemic, from 1885 to about 1895, people considered cocaine to be nonaddictive. Similar pronouncements were made during the decade of the 1970's, a period during which cocaine use remained isolated, a subcultural phenomenon involving only select groups. From 1885 to 1895, there was a proliferation of products containing cocaine. This was prior to the control acts that would eventually prohibit these products from entering the marketplace. Cocaine was an ingredient of products ranging from "Coca Cola" to toothache drops. There was even a product called dope; cocaine was called dope in the early movies about cocaine. Pope Leo XIII endorsed cocaine. So did Jules Verne. Three thousand physicians wrote endorsements of Vin Miriani wine, a wine preparation containing cocaine. People took cocaine for depression, upset stomach, even for tuberculosis.

Gradually, beginning in the late 1800's, perceptions of cocaine and the social climate governing the acceptance of its use began to change. People began questioning the benefits of the drug and they became more aware of its addictive and destructive potential. New medical data and interpretations began to appear. In the medical journals there were reports of overdoses and deaths from cocaine. Finally, legislation was created which said, in essence, that this substance is very dangerous and shouldn't be used without careful medical supervision and control.

Between 1920, the year when the earlier cocaine epidemic abated, and 1970, we apparently forgot the destructive impact that cocaine earlier had on our culture. In the 1970's we rediscovered the drug and ignored the problems that cocaine caused during the earlier epidemic. Large numbers of people who began using cocaine this time were adult children of addictive parents foundering in a world that values external symbols and demands the right answers to questions like: "How much money do you make?" "How big is your house?" They furiously labored to achieve all of these things, perhaps working ten or twelve hours a day, some discovering cocaine as a power source.

The period of the 1980's seems to parallel that shift in the perception of the hazards of the drug that occurred at the turn of the century. We have been repeatedly exposed to reports of prominent figures, like Lenny Bias, dying from using cocaine. We're seeing more articles appear in the medical and psychological journals about the problems of cocaine. State governments are considering or implementing more severe punishments for cocaine distributors.

Dr. Welti, a toxicologist, talks about how Miami reached the point where there were an average of two deaths a week–overdose deaths–attributed to cocaine. In southeast Texas, people are appalled by weekly reports of suicides stemming from the use of crack and rock cocaine. In Washington, D.C. there is the national disgrace of the drug wars whose casualties each year exceed the entire casualty figures for the Palestinian uprising to date.

An increased awareness of the serious personal and societal threat of cocaine addiction has provided the impetus in the workplace for the testing of urine for drugs. This is a new technology, of course, which was unavailable during earlier periods of our history. At the community level, organizations such as PRIDE have attempted to heighten awareness that cocaine is a horrible chemical. All this is reminiscent of the late 1800's, when it was proclaimed that cocaine was the third scourge of mankind, right after alcohol and morphine.

If the earlier epidemic's prevalence curve were to be repeated, we would expect to see a sharp decline in the use of cocaine by the year 2000. However, this projection may be over-optimistic because there is a major force counteracting positive social trends: a more readily available, higher impact cocaine: freebase, rock and crack.

In addition, widespread and sophisticated marketing and a major economic subsystem built around cocaine production and distribution must all be considered wild cards in any attempts at forecasting the future.

The progress of the cocaine epidemic has major implications for treatment planning. If this was an alcohol epidemic, it might take ten, fifteen, or even twenty years for a person to reach an addictive state requiring professional treatment. However, with the known progression curve of cocaine addiction, it may require only from six months to four or five years of freebase smoking to put a person in a position where he's lost home, family, job, health, and maybe had some legal problems. This means that at least through the 1990's there will be a strong and growing demand for professional treatment.

Producing Cocaine Hydrochloride

In the mid-1800's we discovered how to isolate a potent, crystalline, white powder from the coca leaf. The coca leaf in its natural form is about one percent cocaine, but we learned how to refine the leaf material into a ninety-nine percent pure white powder. We learned that the powder could be introduced into our bodies by injecting it as a solution or by snorting it through the nose. We discovered that if we injected a cocaine solution, the drug would reach our brain in about fourteen seconds. If snorted, it would get there in about three to four minutes. If we chewed it, fifteen or twenty minutes would elapse before an effect was felt. That effect was mild, like coffee.

Looking at the source of cocaine, the coca bush, about one percent of the leaf's weight comprises its active ingredient. Cocaine is found naturally in a form called an alkaloid. Alkaloid means "something like" an alkaline substance. (On some Mondays we're "humanoids"–more or less human). As an alkaline-like substance, cocaine has a high pH index.

The problem with alkaloidal cocaine is that if you try to snort or inject it, about a quart of water is required to dissolve one gram. To inject alkaloidal cocaine, you'd need a syringe big enough to hold a quart of water. You'd probably die of over-hydration before you could get the drug into your system. This is impractical. Snorting alkaloidal cocaine would be like packing mud up your nose. It wouldn't dissolve well.

So, modern chemistry is applied. From basic chemistry we know that if we add an acid, in this case hydrochloric acid, to an alkaloid, we get a salt–cocaine hydrochloride. Cocaine hydrochloride is highly water soluble. You can take ten or twelve drops of water, put them in a gram of cocaine hydrochloride, and have a perfectly clear solution.

Most of the cocaine that has been smuggled into the United States during recent years has been in the form of cocaine hydrochloride, processed in the kitchens of Peru, Ecuador, Bolivia or Columbia. Cocaine hydrochloride is suitable for snorting or injecting, but we still have a problem. It's difficult to smoke, the fastest and most direct method of getting a drug to the brain.

How Cocaine is Administered

Few people take or "drop" cocaine orally. We can't digest it and pass it into our systems efficiently, like food. It works poorly that way. The acids in the stomach don't degrade the cocaine, and the "high impact" potency of the drug is virtually lost. Also, oral administration produces a slow onset of effect. There would be no rush, the experience sought by cocaine users.

The most common way of administering cocaine is by the intranasal route. It takes the drug three to four minutes to get from nose to brain. It must first penetrate the mucous membrane, a rate-limiting step. It must dissolve in water, get into the mucous membrane, go into the veins, the vena cava, the right side of the heart, then be pumped through the lungs to the left side of the heart and out to the brain and body. Additional time is required for the drug to get into the brain and produce an effect.

When you inject cocaine into your arm with a hypodermic syringe, what happens is a little different. The same basic route comes into play, but the cocaine travels from arm to brain in about fourteen seconds. It goes into the veins, the vena cava, the right side of the heart, the lungs, back to the left heart and up into the brain.

I once thought that the most impactful way to get any drug into the system was to inject it. I also thought that injecting was the most dangerous way to get drugs into the system. With freebasing, which I'll describe later, neither statement is true.

People who injected cocaine, back in the late 1960's and early 1970's, would inject half of their cocaine, wait a few seconds and see if "the bells came out." Are you familiar with a sixties dance called the "hucklebuck?" When people become toxic from cocaine and start getting close to overdose, they start doing the hucklebuck. You can't hear; you start strobing. You can't see, and your body starts to shake.

I was talking to a man and we were comparing war stories. He said, "You know, when I started to get the hucklebuck, when I was shooting up in the early seventies, that was the point I wanted to be at. I always had to be careful when I got that toxic because I didn't want to give myself too much. So I would put half the cocaine in and wait a little while. When I started to shake, if I could still get the other half in I would put it in. If I couldn't, just from my arm motion, I would usually throw the syringe across the room. Then I would always be on the floor. There would be a moment of truth. I wanted to know if it was the room shaking or me shaking. So I had a little mirror that I put right down on floor level. And I would look over there and see that, yes, it was me doing the hucklebuck, and yes, it was where I wanted to be." That is bordering on seizure, bordering on extreme overdose. That's the crazy thrill and rush. That's where people can get when they're injecting cocaine.

Freebasing, or smoking, cocaine results in acutely high blood levels of the drug. When a person freebases, inhales cocaine vapors into the lungs, cocaine is hitting the brain in only six to eight seconds. It by-passes the right side of heart and lungs and goes straight to the left heart and out to the brain. Freebase is rapidly increasing in popularity. Many people start out using cocaine intranasally and then progress to freebasing. However, with recent changes in the packaging and distribution of cocaine, many youth now begin their involvement with cocaine by smoking it in the form of rock or crack.

Cocaine has been smoked in South America for years in the form of coca paste, a cocaine sulfate. We called it base. In South America, the paste smoked is about thirty percent cocaine. Nevertheless, smoking paste is now the leading cause of psychiatric admission in Columbia. Cocaine in its base form, right out of the coca plant, is more the alkaloid or pure product. You heat it to a lower temperature to vaporize it. In other words, it is more volatile than cocaine hydrochloride. With cocaine in its base form, and a good pipe, you are getting about fifty percent of the cocaine into your system.

The main import into this country, however, is cocaine hydrochloride. To smoke the cocaine that is available we had to find a way to change its characteristics, to "convert" it. One of the things you'll find in chemistry books is that it takes intense heat to make cocaine hydrochloride, a very stable compound, go from a solid, flaky, white material into a gas—a process termed sublimation. It requires a temperature of approximately 359 degrees Fahrenheit. At this high temperature, much of the cocaine is destroyed.

To avoid destroying the costly drug, it is better to convert the cocaine hydrochloride back into its alkaloid form. In its alkaloid form, cocaine will vaporize at approximately 209 degrees Fahrenheit. We've found many creative ways to make this conversion. One way to think about freebase is to look at the equation or formula for cocaine hydrochloride, and imagine freeing the alkaloidal cocaine from the hydrochloride salt. This returns the substance to its original alkaloid form that will vaporize at only 209 degrees. Most of the cocaine is retained during the conversion and the end product will produce that euphoric, eight-second rush when smoked.

The terms we hear on the street for freebase are rock or crack. I first heard the term rock in the Oakland/Los Angeles area. The term crack seems to have come from the cracking sound that freebase cocaine makes when you "torch it," or heat it, so it goes from a solid state to a gaseous state for inhalation.

The old way of making this conversion was the Richard Pryor method, using ether. The problem with ether is that it is flammable. Ether is also heavier than air and dissipates slowly. If you put a can of ether on the table, its vapors will fall and creep along the floor. And it takes a lot of minutes for your area to ventilate enough to light a match safely. Richard Pryor talks about his freebase experience, where he set himself on fire. The accident happened while trying to light a freebase pipe with ether still in the air. This story, however, has changed over time. Richard now describes the event as a suicide attempt, possibly related to his use of freebase. The federal government has started to regulate the sales of ether, so it is not as readily available now as it once was. But we found we could use other ubiquitous solvents to make the conversion. For example you could take things right out of mom's pantry, like baking soda, or go into the laundry room and get ammonia bleach, or ammonia.

Baking soda or ammonia can be used to reverse the equation I mentioned earlier, taking cocaine hydrochloride back to the alkaloid. We invented a simple conversion process called "shake and bake." One way to do this is to get a little plastic container, put in the cocaine hydrochloride dissolved in water, add ammonia, shake it up, and use a double boiler or other heat source to catalyze the reaction. What precipitates, or coagulates, is the alkaloidal form of cocaine. This is dried out and sold in little hunks or rocks, or in larger rectangular shapes called slabs.

I was sitting in my office with a mother and her fifteen and sixteen-year-old adolescent children. She was concerned about her children, drugs, all the strange friends they were hanging around, their school performance, and that things were just not going well for the family. She described all these problems and finally said, " . . . and on top of that, both of my kids got microwaves and none of them cook in their rooms." Well, the kids were using the microwaves for the heat to catalyze this reaction, a process known as "nuking the cocaine." So the kids were nuking the cocaine. And when mom said that, both the kids almost crawled under their chairs. I mean they knew it was "up"–they'd been exposed. They were both using microwave ovens to catalyze the reaction and rapidly dry the cocaine for smoking.

Manufacturing smokeable cocaine has become less hazardous in terms of not having to worry about blowing yourself up. There are even kits that can be purchased with solvents in them. These kits, bought at "head" shops or through the mail, produce base cocaine with a purity as high as ninety-five to ninety-seven and one-half percent. People are dying from it because it is so potent. We are seeing two hundred to three hundred percent increases in overdoses in major urban areas across the country from freebase.

A water pipe is an instrument often used to smoke cocaine–the same type of water pipe that came out of the '60's marijuana culture. There is liquid in the pipe and a little receptacle for the cocaine. You use a torch to light it. The torch can be a lighter or a match, or sometimes a coat hanger and a little piece of cotton ball soaked in 151 proof rum. The cocaine vapor is sucked in through the pipe, through the liquid. The liquid may be wine; it may be Corvoissier cognac; it may be 151 proof rum (depending upon your preference). You inhale this gas directly into your mouth and lungs.

Another way of freebasing is to simply use a straight, heat resistant tube. People put the rock in the tube, heat it, and inhale the gases directly into the lungs. Straight pipe users should worry about possible lung damage. With the water pipe you have a cooling system and a filtration system. With the straight pipe you're getting nothing but a straight, unfiltered, hot gas into your lungs and throat. These organs are unsuited for handling that intense heat.

Another device commonly used for freebasing is a tin can crushed on one side to create a "bowl" effect,

There are several physical hazards to smoking cocaine. We know from the Len Bias story that cocaine can kill. We know that some people display violent physical reactions to cocaine and can die the first time they use it. We know that other people will have changes in their tolerance to the drug, a process we call kindling. Kindling is a form of changing tolerance where from one week to the next people may not know how well they will tolerate their customary levels of cocaine use.

Experts seem to agree that if someone continues to inhale a hot gas with all sorts of breakdown products into their lungs, early chronic obstructive lung disease is likely to occur. We may see the early onset of emphysema in some of the adolescents and young adults who are starting to use rock and crack cocaine.

Another problem was brought to my attention when I had the opportunity to talk with Dr. Welti, a toxicologist and medical examiner from the Miami area. Dr. Welti, mentioned that upon autopsy, he was seeing adolescents and young adults whose coronary arteries looked like they were fifty to sixty years old. He said the process of smoking cocaine can cause a narrowing of the coronary arteries. Injecting cocaine may produce similar damage. It may be transient narrowing, but somehow the body is interpreting it as damage. The linings of the inside of those arteries are getting more and more occluded. We expect to see some cardiovascular problems arising at an early age in the cocaine-using population.

People who freebase or use cocaine intravenously (I.V.) are usually more out of control. If you're an adolescent down in Florida and you're losing your mind on cocaine or crack, they call you a "crack monster." Although you have people who intranasally use large amounts of the drug, the severity of its impact on the central nervous system, compared with freebase and I.V., is less profound. You cannot assimilate enough cocaine through snorting to match the blood levels in the brain you get from freebase and I.V.

For example, if you go out and snort a few grams or an eight-ball (eighth of an ounce), you may achieve a blood level of two hundred to four hundred nanogram percent. That is the peak. If you go out and freebase a quarter of an ounce, or an ounce, you could display one thousand to twelve hundred nanogram percent blood level. This is an increase of three to six times the blood level of the drug. Therefore, you infer that there is significant impact on the brain's thought and emotional processes. There may be greater distortion. I also think that the lifestyles of people who use cocaine intravenously, or who freebase, become radically different from those of social snorters.

Marketing Cocaine

We notice that it was the post-World War II baby boom generation, people now in their thirties and forties, who introduced cocaine in the 1960's and 1970's. They were the primary consumers. But like the heroin addict who matures out in his middle to late thirties, we started to see some maturing out of middle-aged, cocaine-addicted individuals. Thus, the market for cocaine began to flatten out in terms of escalating numbers.

If we were involved in the business of making money from cocaine we might think, "What population of people could we sell cocaine to, making a better buck?" Well, I think it's obvious. We have a brand new consumer line right now, a product that hits quick–freebase–and we can develop that and sell it to a young market. To sell it to a young market we do exactly what pharmaceutical companies do: unit dose it.

Crack and rock cocaine, or freebase cocaine, is marketed to a younger population. The targeted market is youth ranging in age from twelve to thirty. These are the primary consumers of crack and rock, the market the product is designed for. Unit dosing has brought price structure changes that make cocaine available even to youth with limited funds. Five or ten years ago, if we wanted to go out and "party like crazy and grab some cocaine," we had to come up with about one hundred dollars for a gram. If I was fifteen years old and I had one hundred dollars in my pocket (which is highly unlikely), I would face a big choice. I could drink for a month or more. Or, I could smoke reefer for a month. But to spend one hundred dollars on a white substance I've never tried, and that would only last for an evening–that was an unlikely choice. Also, the purity of the product was poor, and we looked at cocaine as a narcotic–a dangerous street drug.

With a one-unit dose of rock or crack cocaine costing as little as two-fifty, no higher than ten dollars, cocaine becomes attractive to youth. At these prices, crack or rock is within their financial means. Incidentally, on the surface it appears that crack cocaine is cheap. Crack cocaine is no cheaper than snorting cocaine. You will pay a fractional, but proportionate price of bulk cocaine. You see, it takes several rocks, perhaps ten, to make a gram (depending on the size of the rocks), and at ten dollars a rock you're still paying one hundred dollars a gram. These figures change according to the "going price" of cocaine but the relationship remains stable. It's not cheaper, it just appears cheaper. In the long run it will be more expensive because of the high doses that people use in their love affair with cocaine.

In terms of product lines coming into this country, we're seeing an influx of preprocessed crack or rock. We know, for example, that just about the only product line you can get through the Bahamas is rock or crack: free-baseable, smokeable cocaine. Often we're seeing home laboratories or small "set-ups" that take cocaine hydrochloride and convert it–a new "cottage industry."

Cocaine prices obey the economic laws of supply and demand. The street price of cocaine averages between sixty and one hundred dollars per gram at the time of this writing. In rural Ohio you may still have to pay one hundred dollars or more to score a gram of cocaine, while in Miami, Florida you can get cocaine in gram portions, that may be as high as seventy to ninety percent pure, for fifty to sixty dollars. Right now it's a buyer's market. Everyone is saying that the cocaine glut is just starting. With a cocaine glut, prices are down and quality is up.

A few years ago when you saw crack cocaine or a base rock, you could be sure it was pure, without adulterants. But now we're starting to see quality control problems in rock and crack cocaine. You don't know what's in it. You can find all sorts of things in there. We're seeing cuts in rock and crack. These are techniques for expanding weight and volume and adding other drugs for impact. For example, some people have been adding drain cleaner to rock and crack processing to increase weight, volume and profits. If you look at what the adolescent consumer buys, the powdered type of the drug is still hit-and-miss. Often it isn't cocaine. It could be several different things from PCP to caffeine, to a little amphetamine, to nothing more than just an inert white powder. When we see rock or crack, however, it is usually purer. But there is the growing potential of added adulterants.

The product line is changing, too. Combinations of drugs are being sold to cocaine users, complicating the addiction picture. Rock and crack are not only unit-dosed but are sometimes sold in what is called a "slab." You can buy three or more different hits in a slab. A slab may be pure cocaine, ninety-seven percent, or it could be cut with PCP (called space base), or heroin (like a speedball used in the heroin culture). In Texas they call the PCP-cocaine polydrug "Dusty Rhodes." Cocaine is being laced with amphetamine ("crank") in many areas of the country.

Another drug which has surfaced in the last few years is "basuco." This product was originally a type of smokeable cocaine that was used mainly in South America. Its purity was relatively low, being about thirty or forty percent cocaine. Its remaining composition includes sulfuric acid, a dangerous substance which is a by-product of the refining process. More and more of this is entering the United States today.

Sometimes these drug combinations, for example the classic "speedball," are designed to minimize a particular side effect. The classic speedball is cocaine with heroin, usually injected. Cocaine and heroin can now be smoked together, sometimes referred to as "chasing the dragon." Today it's a buyer's market and sellers are sensitive to the types of drugs people want. There are sophisticated marketing schemes.

In Miami, for instance, someone said, "Look, we had a big report that said cocaine causes a reduction in vitamins B and C." We soon began to pick up cocaine that was laced with vitamins B and C. Another paper came out that said people who snort cocaine end up with sinus infections; there was bacteria in the cocaine. Soon, cases turned up where people came into emergency rooms with an allergic reaction to the penicillin found in their cocaine.

Cocaine, the drug, is not a singular, unique commodity. It is produced in a variety of ways, with an assortment of adulterants, many of which are in and of themselves very harmful. To compound this variety, the drug is consumed in a number of different ways.

The purveyors of cocaine have met the varying demands of the market with a flexible array of products, product units and selling techniques, all designed to supply cocaine to the widest possible audience. Furthermore, just as the drug, its consumption, and its marketing have expanded and increased in a relatively short time, it is reasonable to assume that this pattern of growth will continue.

Who, then, are the users of cocaine? Chapter 3 looks at the consumers of the drug, the customers of the mega-business of cocaine, and their dependence upon it.

Chapter 3

COCAINE DEPENDENCE

Andrew Wiel, in *Chocolate to Morphine*, says there is nothing wrong with drugs. They are neither inherently good nor bad. People use them for reasons that often lead to serious problems, creating bad relationships between the consumer and the drug. Tragically, that appears to be the norm when the drug is cocaine.

I was in Connecticut lecturing on cocaine, intimacy, and sexual relationships. I noticed a lady crying in the audience. During the break I took her aside and said, "What happened? It seems there's something occurring in your life related to what we're talking about." She said, "Yes, my husband is a doctor and he just picked cocaine over me. We're getting a divorce."

I hear this a lot. "Cocaine can't hug me or kiss me; it can't give me affection. Yet I will pick this damned white substance over people who can do all the nice things in the world for me. I pick it over my job. Pick it over anything. Half of the time, I pick it over sex–but I would prefer to have sex with it."

This is cocaine addiction and it simply means we're saying, "This person can't stop." I've often asked patients who were cocaine addicts, "What do you think about this stuff? Do you think it causes physical dependency?" The reply has generally been, "I used to think cocaine wasn't physically addictive but when, for the thousandth time, I tried but couldn't stop using it, I figured I had a problem. Maybe I was dependent."

When you ask people who use cocaine regularly if they have a dependency problem, what you hear is, "Yes, I do, because I can't stop. Even when I want to stop, I can't stop. Nine out of ten times I can't refuse cocaine. Nine out of ten times, even when I don't want to use cocaine, just being physically close to it causes me to use again. If I take one line, I'll take every bit I can get my hands on. I may even start calling people at 4 A.M. to get more."

Alcohol and cocaine dependents share the same patterns of initial reactions to the drug experience. Cocaine dependents often say, "I remember a time when I thought I could never do more than a half or one gram of cocaine a night." Then there are those who are immediately captivated, who "get down" in their first episode. With cocaine, however, the progression of the drug dependency is different from alcohol.

An alcoholic may spend from five to thirty years developing the addiction we call alcoholism, all the psychological, behavioral, social, spiritual problems of chemical dependency. With adolescents freebasing cocaine, we see a progression to a situation requiring intensive treatment in from two to six months. With adults, we're seeing anywhere from six months to three or four years of heavy use, to develop the same levels and types of difficulties it takes twenty years for chronic alcoholics to develop.

Dr. Doug Talbot, a well known addictionologist, believes there is a drug dependency progression that occurs within the brain itself. When a person starts using drugs, conscious choice governs. The cerebral cortex, the computer part of the brain, enables this person to turn off the drug use early, get to bed, and do the things he needs to do. But as drug use continues, something happens so that the person becomes dependent upon the drug, physiologically and psychologically.

Dr. Talbot believes what happens is that at some point the drug takes on a property which the brain interprets as an instinct, something necessary for survival. After watching my father die of alcoholism and others die of addiction, this is the only explanation that makes sense to me. The drug's having taken on an instinctive quality equated with survival is the only way I can explain the behaviors I see among cocaine addicts.

Related to the inability to stop is the inability to conserve the drug, to put some away for tomorrow. This is also true of people who have become dependent upon marijuana, heroin, alcohol, tranquilizers, sedatives, and the "Heinz 57" variety of drugs that alter consciousness. Why is it when people become chemically dependent they can't leave a little bit for tomorrow? It's rare to find a cocaine addict who is going to save any at all. They say things like this to themselves: "I have two grams left and I want to put some of it away." They can't bring themselves to do it though. The anguish of coming off this drug and the strong components of addiction involved in using cocaine make it practically impossible for dependents to conserve.

The *Diagnostic and Statistical Manual* of the American Psychiatric Association (The *DSM-III*) declares cocaine abstinence a disorder that induces people to use cocaine because the dysphoria or anguish of coming off this drug is profound. When you are getting off a drug like alcohol, you are coming down for several hours. Distributing the experience of coming down over several hours doesn't seem to result in the intense anguish of cocaine abstinence. Cocaine "takes you up" quickly, but drops you quickly too. If it hits your brain within six to eight seconds, in the time it takes to get the freebase pipe from your mouth to the table, you experience a "coming down" that is also precipitous.

Coming off cocaine is one of the most anguished, depressing experiences. I've watched people talk about coming off freebase and one of the things I noticed was the nonverbal maneuvers they use to describe it. It looks like they're describing a heart attack. They have fists clenched to the chest. You can see that it hurts. They can recreate that hurt for you because it's a devastating event. They'll do almost anything to keep from crashing on cocaine. And on top of that they'll do just about anything to keep their supply coming. Postcocaine anguish is a strong inducement to use again–to keep the pain away.

There are moral and legal issues pertaining to using cocaine. It is an illegal drug. This raises serious questions about the notion of the "recreational use" of cocaine. From a clinical perspective it is difficult to answer the question, "What is recreational cocaine use?" Are there people who can use cocaine without experiencing trouble with it? There may be a subpopulation of people who can "do a little bit" of cocaine, put it away, "do a little bit more later," and not have problems. But therapists and counselors don't have people coming to them saying, "I snorted two lines of cocaine last night. Can you help me? I enjoyed the hell out of it." The people may be out there somewhere but they aren't part of the clinical scene. The cocaine users whom therapists and counselors see are those who have lost families, health, jobs and hope. They are victims of a progressive addiction.

Unfortunately, some of the basic reference materials used by psychologists, psychiatrists and other clinicians in the past, for example the *DSM-III* mentioned earlier, described cocaine as a substance of abuse—but not a substance of dependence. A recent edition of this manual, *DSM III-R*, describes cocaine as a drug of dependence producing potential. The notion is that you can distinguish between the mind and the body, and that the crucial issue is what happens to the body. Dependence is a physical phenomenon. But I don't think you can differentiate the mind from the body. In terms of consequences for the drug user, his family and the community, what difference does it make if his destruction has arisen from a psychological dependence or from a physical dependence? The truth is, he can't stop using cocaine and is in desperate trouble.

I have worked with people who have used cocaine for less than a year and whose lives were already shattered. One gentleman in particular comes to mind. In nine months he had blown $150,000, had lost his whole family, owed another $50,000, and was in an auto wreck. He had blown everything . . . from job to family. The progressive nature of the illness is astonishing.

I am convinced, from my work with drug users, that cocaine causes both psychological and physiological dependence, just as alcohol, Valium and many other drugs do. We see consistent patterns of electroencephalogram changes and biochemical changes, and we repeatedly observe the same set of symptoms in early recovery. These facts tell me that cocaine is a chemical which causes physical dependency.

Personality, Temperament and Addiction

Your personality and temperament are a major influence on your choice of drugs and how you use them. With or without drugs, I've found that people repeat the behaviors that produce the neural transmissions they want to feel. For me, lecturing produces some of the same excitement and thrill that cocaine did. So I choose to do it. Think about it. I started to lecture about twelve years ago, within a few years of giving up cocaine. Lecturing remains a thrilling experience. I get that anticipatory excitement before I come out to speak to a group. I love it. I crave it. I don't think I will ever change. I don't think I will ever be a person who doesn't like stimulation.

I know of no technique that will let me take a cocaine person, who loves excitement, and say, "Okay, now you don't like excitement any more. Now you just want to be middle-of-the-road. You don't like the cutting edge anymore. Now put that in your mind. Get off the street where you can make a thousand a week with new Reeboks and sweets and just get a job for minimum wage." It just doesn't work. So what I have to start thinking of is that I want that cocaine dependent to experience excitement, but I want it to be appropriate. I want him to get his thrills in ways that do not result in problems.

With the woman's husband who chose cocaine over her, we have a physician who found, through experimentation, a chemical and a set of behaviors that met a perceived need. Are there any general statements or rules that apply here? I think so. However, no general system that tries to explain drug-related behavior fits every case. You can usually come up with cases that challenge any system. Nevertheless, I have found it useful to consider people's coping styles together with how they "tie into" drug use patterns. I have been impressed by the consistent relationships between coping style and gravitation to stimulants or depressants.

Imagine that you are an adolescent or young adult. You've learned that in seconds you can feel better. Then I'd like you to imagine that one day someone said to you, "You really shouldn't use cocaine. You should find a softer, easier way of living. You should find a better, healthier way of life. Maybe you should try Narcotics Anonymous or Cocaine Anonymous or Alcoholics Anonymous. The next time you feel lonely, or isolated, or depressed, instead of picking up that freebase pipe that will make you feel better in six to eight seconds, why don't you just go to a meeting?" This instead of six seconds to instant gratification for a brain that has learned that it can feel better?

People who use central nervous system depressants—alcohol, opiates, tranquilizers, sleeping pills, and pot—tend to cope with stress through isolation and relaxation. It's an avoidance dynamic. It is a "take in to keep down." What do depressants do? They reduce neural transmissions in the brain. Take a person functioning at his typical level. If he wants to shut out internal dialogue or "chatter in the head," wants to shut out a lot of stimulation, consider the effect of two or three ten-milligram Valium and a shot of heroin. It reduces the number of neural transmissions in the brain. He won't be thinking about much because there won't be a whole lot of neural firing there. People who want to go on a true honeymoon and end up in a vacuum, "shoot heroin." They think about nothing then.

I find that people who use stimulant drugs want to confront a hostile environment with intellectual or physical activity. It is more of an arousal model. They need to be in control. They need to be on the cutting edge. They need to be able to "deal with" the situation. I find that they jump in, both feet first, even when they don't know what they're doing. These are the general differences I see between people who use depressants and stimulants.

Self-medication

I believe compulsive use of a chemical can be seen as an attempt at self-medication. Every client I've seen, even if psychotic, sought and usually found a drug to help deal with existential problems. People learn what to take in to make themselves feel better. We find that people learn how to self-medicate. To understand how people function as their own pharmacologists, Andrew Wiel's book, *The Natural Mind*, is an excellent resource. Finding the drug that works for us isn't a random process. We search until we find one that provides the relief we seek.

Drugs can help us cope with a feeling or a problem–people, places and things that we don't handle well. Whenever I talk to someone about a chemical dependency problem I ask, "What did you get out of this drug? What is the good part of it?" "Oh, it made me feel good. It made me feel like I was one of the crowd. When I had cocaine in my pocket all the chicks really dug me. I always had a lot of friends, and before that I was always a very lonely person." Anyone who wants to help the person with a drug problem must listen carefully to the answers to these questions.

The drug user is getting something from the drug that is perceived as valuable. I have observed clients prefer drugs that help them cope with the feelings that trouble them the most. I think that to a great degree the "feeling" problems dictate drug choice more than the "people, places, and things" problems. People experiment with a whole range of drugs to find the one that best suits their own unique psychological needs.

Often, cocaine addicts use drugs to self-medicate the side effects of the cocaine itself. Typically, as cocaine use escalates, so does the use of depressants. It's almost a universal phenomenon. The reason is that cocaine has some very negative side effects. You walk around with your muscles tight and tense, with your jaws clenched, with your heart rate at 120, 130, 140 a minute, and with a blood pressure of 200-and-something over about 160. Then there are the paranoid thoughts: rigid, repetitive, obsessive, compulsive types of behavior–thinking that every time a car goes by it's a police officer so I better look out here and make sure it's not. There may be seizures. You may hear clients come in at this stage and say, "You know, I've had a seizure before and I really don't want to quit using cocaine. Can you just give me some phenobarbital and dilantin?" So maybe I can use some prophylactic medication to try to keep from having a seizure. They don't want to quit using, so they're entering another level of self-medicating.

The Polydrug Complication

People who work with clients in chemical dependency programs believe in abstinence from all drugs. However, in dealing with cocaine dependence we often hear clients claim that cocaine is the only chemical they've had trouble with. While they may perceive cocaine as undesirable and a source of extreme problems, they don't want to forego the other drugs they use. They say, "Cocaine is the only thing I ever lost control over in my whole life. You see, I've been drinking for ten years and smoking pot for fifteen years. I never had a problem with that. So don't tell me I'm going to have to give that up, too."

That is the first hurdle in the struggle to help the cocaine addict recover from his illness. Do we keep the cocaine dependent in treatment even while he uses other drugs, or do we tell him to go out there and come back when things get bad enough? Perhaps the client has been involved with other counselors, one of whom said, "Okay, we're going to monitor your drinking and we're going to set up indicators of things that are out of control." When even one "authority" gives tacit approval of drinking, the cocaine addict will use this to try to persuade others to approve also.

Usually when a cocaine addict says, "But you can't take away the alcohol and pot because they were never a problem," he has a poor perception of his actual drug consumption. What I have found is that their perception of their own alcohol and pot consumption predates their heavy cocaine use. Their model of how much is drunk or smoked may be one, two, or even five years old. It isn't current. One of the things you must do is capture the truth and drive it home.

First, I do a drug and alcohol history. A few days later I do a psychosocial history. Then I collapse the two together and say, "My, isn't this interesting. It looks like, as you escalated in your drug use, you also escalated in your psychosocial problems. And there also appears to be some escalation in the alcohol and pot use." This is an issue you will run into again and again.

Working toward acceptance of the polydrug problem should lead patients to the realization that they cannot use drugs of any kind. Cocaine addiction has been devastating. They owe money. They have lost almost everything they loved. They are in therapy, depressed, and extremely dysphoric, and yet there is a big piece of them that would like to use cocaine. They know that maybe they can't. But they remain unwilling to face the issues of alcohol and pot.

If a cocaine addict continues to use alcohol and pot, he will continue to use very poor judgment. And probably he will return to cocaine use. I have worked with clients on an outpatient basis, allowing them to define for themselves what out-of-control means in terms of pot and alcohol use. We have monitored drug use/abuse and I've kept them in treatment this way. When things start to go wrong, we begin working with the other addictions. Every therapist and treatment program must deal with this issue of control.

Psychiatric Disorders

Sometimes a client doesn't fit your model of what a typical cocaine addict should look like. For example, I had a cocaine addict who was toxic and came in somewhat psychotic. He was having delusions and was in a paranoid state. He said, "I know that you people have planted a little radio in my molar, and that everyone in the waiting room can hear everything I am thinking."

This isn't a typical presentation of someone who is toxic and paranoid from cocaine. It is a typical presentation of schizophrenia. Schizophrenic is what this person was. Probably ten percent or more of those seeking treatment for cocaine dependence have psychiatric disorders. There is a relationship cited in the psychological literature suggesting that people who have certain psychological or psychiatric problems gravitate toward cocaine. There is also, however, the cocaine dependent who begins to show symptoms of psychiatric disorders arising from the overuse of the drug itself.

A typical scenario I encounter in treating cocaine addicts is one where the person begins to show signs of schizophrenia. This addict has often been on a chronic binge for as much as a week without sleeping or eating, and taking in very little fluid–just putting cocaine into the system. The result is some pretty bizarre behaviors, with hallucinations being the most universal. We may see the onset of a paranoid-schizophrenia type of presentation.

One of the facts lost in the history of psychiatry was that morphine products were used in Europe for a number of years to treat schizophrenia. It was used fairly effectively in treating the acute symptoms of schizophrenia. Morphine can knock someone right out of a psychotic episode. Heroin will do the same thing. But it doesn't work as a treatment for schizophrenia resulting from cocaine toxicity because it produces a secondary addiction and an even more complicated treatment profile. But cocaine addicts often discover that opiates and depressants help mitigate the schizophrenia-like side effects of cocaine toxicity and when this happens, the cocaine use escalates even further. You will also see an increase in the amount of alcohol used, often in combination with benzodiazepenes, Valium, Librium, and other tranquilizers. In some cases you'll see the use of sleeping pills, the opiates–anything from demerol and dilaudid to heroin and morphine. You'll see increased marijuana smoking, although marijuana has a biphasic effect. What this means is that although when a cocaine addict first smokes a joint he's likely to feel stimulated–feel his heart pounding or have premature ventricular contraction–but over a period of time it will begin to have a sedative effect.

When we consider this scenario of intense cocaine use, we must be concerned about the interactive effects of the other drugs which start to appear in the abusive pattern.

It is crucial to gain accurate information about the other drugs that are being used by the cocaine addict, especially an alcohol/Valium combination, if we are considering an outpatient treatment. This is where we begin to encounter life-threatening withdrawal. I'm also extremely concerned about any of the drugs besides alcohol, especially the benzodiazepenes and barbiturates, that may cause seizure or delirium tremens types of conditions resulting in an medical emergency or death.

In trying to gain insight into the question of if and how psychiatric disorders are involved in a client's cocaine addiction, one of the things I ask is, "What were your subjective experiences when you first used cocaine? What was it like the first time?" Usually the feeling was arousal because cocaine is a central nervous system stimulant. Then, after about forty-five minutes to one hour, the person returns to his or her original state. There may be a slight dysphoric rebound. I've had several patients who ended up with severe depression problems tell me they had a more pronounced rebound. This may be only a slight indicator, but it is something I've become sensitive to.

Other psychiatric problems common among cocaine addicts are bipolar disorders, attention-deficiency disorders, cyclothymic disorders, and clinical depression. Of these, depression appears to be the most prevalent.

In the cocaine population you may find some preexisting chronic depression. When I start to see someone who has these features, I want to know about the family history and any depressive episodes that may have occurred in the past. I will want to do a thorough history to document whether depressive episodes existed before the onset of cocaine usage.

The other phenomenon I see is cocaine users fitting the model of bipolar illness—those who are manic-depressive. This condition must always be verified or ruled out, if suspected. This is to make sure that a psychiatric problem isn't going to become part of the problem once we begin treating the cocaine addiction. In cases where there is more pathology than just the addiction, we must treat the multiple conditions in a parallel fashion. If people find a drug that meets some of their needs, both biochemical and psychological, the use of that drug is doubly entrenched.

Treating the addiction without treating the depression or other psychiatric problems is doomed to fail. As soon as you treat their cocaine problem, addicts may become profoundly depressed. What are they going to think about? What type of craving are they going to have? I think when we consider these problems we begin to understand the bonds between psychiatric disorders and drug addiction.

Although cocaine dependency is a complex disorder posing serious challenges to treatment, the longer I work with cocaine addicts the more I appreciate that they are just like anyone else. They have the potential to be wonderful people. They are fun to work with and they do recover.

Five years ago, I walked around to anyone who would listen to me saying, "There is hope in treating the cocaine addict." Now, I think we have the technology, if we have the understanding and the will, to treat the cocaine addict as effectively as we treat any other addict. Probably the only exception to this optimistic statement would be the population whose addictive profile is similar to that of the inner city heroine addict, the urban freebaser. To treat this person effectively, you must have a massive support system surrounding him. Unfortunately, the environmental support that is required to effectively treat the urban freebaser, especially in the inner city, is rarely available. To create these environmental supports may require several years of committed effort.

I often say the serenity prayer, "God grant me the serenity to accept the things I cannot change, courage to change the things I can, and the wisdom to know the difference." It is widely used as part of recovery programs. In one of my treatment sessions, I asked a cocaine addict to just scribble down what the serenity prayer meant. Instead, he rewrote it and proposed that his version replace the old one. He seemed to think it was much more appropriate. His serenity prayer was, "God grant me the excitement of accepting the few things that I can't control. The wisdom to never miss the chance to control the things I can and the courage to live a straight life."

That prayer says a great deal about where you are starting with a person who is addicted to cocaine. Still, I have never met one who invented a new feeling, a new emotion or a new life problem. If you can show me one cocaine addict that has invented something beyond the emotions written on the little list we use in treatment and a life problem that has not been described by any other addicted person, I will be amazed. I don't think you can. You see, that is what makes all of us the same.

Like the experience and the drug, cocaine dependence is a complex mixture of causes and effects, complicated by the admixture of an array of other drugs–stimulants and depressants. Distinct personality characteristics and psychiatric disorders both presage dependence and accompany it. Nevertheless, treatment holds the potential for successful recovery.

Chapter 4

THE CRISIS

John had reached a point in his cocaine addiction where he was chronically dysphoric–anxious and restless. The only time he felt good, or even normal, was when he was freebasing.

John's family had left weeks ago and he was on the verge of being fired. This didn't concern him as much as the fact he had used all of his family's savings in the last six months, owed nearly five thousand dollars to cocaine dealers and couldn't get cash for more of the drug.

In desperation, John accepted the offer of an acquaintance he had met in a local bar. This person, Mike, had asked John to sell him an ounce of cocaine. Mike had sixteen hundred dollars cash, the money necessary to score such an amount. John, using poor judgment due to his craving for cocaine, consented. He knew he could cut the cocaine and get an eight ball (one-eighth ounce of cocaine) for himself.

John met Mike in a predetermined spot–a grocery store parking lot at a shopping mall. While delivering the cocaine, an unmarked squad car sped to the scene. John had sold cocaine to an undercover police officer.

Only six months ago John had been a respectable, middle class, plant maintenance worker. He had a lovely wife and two beautiful children. Now he had lost his job, family, and perhaps his freedom. But John was fortunate. As part of his sentencing, he was offered treatment and probation as an alternative to jail. The "bust" served as a motivator to force him to seek treatment.

The accidents, the personal losses, the legal problems —all these features can appear with alcoholism, but more gradually and often less intensely than with cocaine addiction. A certain amount of adjustment will occur within the alcoholic's psychosocial environment because the disease's long evolution provides ample time for this to happen. But the personal crisis of the cocaine addict could be called explosive.

Even before a cocaine dependent experiences a personal, or motivational crisis, you begin seeing a life out-of-balance. Most of us, when we are feeling good and our lives are stable, perceive ourselves as having some control over our internal and external environments. When we feel in control, our self-esteem is good. This isn't typical for the cocaine dependent.

For the cocaine dependent, a drug has provided the excitement. In using the drug, he has neglected the everyday details that help maintain home, family, self-respect, or job—the things we perceive as wonderful in our lives. A difficult challenge for treatment is to teach cocaine dependents how to maintain their home, family, self-respect and job while still meeting their needs for excitement and thrills. This is one of the reasons why it is so desirable to get the family involved in the treatment program. I always address this problem in any treatment plan, and work directly with the addict's family whenever it is feasible.

A reversal in control, similar to what I have described, occurs in just about any addiction. The alcoholic experiences a motivational crisis, but the cocaine dependent generally has more legal and financial complications to deal with. The typical cocaine dependent has exhausted vast sums of money. And the loss of money is a motivational factor that will be a big part of what gets him into treatment. You can't do $150,000 worth of alcohol in six months, but you can do that much cocaine. There are people spending five thousand dollars or more per week on cocaine; some do an ounce of cocaine in a day. Freebasing? Sixteen hundred to two thousand dollars a day. At this rate available funds are exhausted fast. Credit is stretched to its limit.

Loss of family, friends and job is a powerful motivator, but even more destabilizing is involvement in illegal and immoral acts to support the cocaine addiction. These activities precipitate agonizing self-reexaminations. For both males and females, prostitution is often involved in supporting cocaine dependency. Whether it is overt or covert, prostitution causes intense feelings of guilt and shame. Being arrested, if you perceive yourself as a middle class citizen, is devastating, too.

Preoccupation with physical complaints is characteristic of the cocaine dependent's first attempts at seeking help. I repeatedly hear questions like, "I had a seizure once, will I have it again? That's all I want to know." Or, "I have a whole bunch of problems breathing through my nose because of snorting cocaine–and what I really want to know is, what is going to happen next?" You see a constellation of physical problems. Seizures are particularly scary and motivating. If they happened once they are likely to happen again, sometimes at lower doses and possibly even after the person has stopped using drugs.

Chronic fatigue, headaches, sore throats—all these physical symptoms are tied to abusing a central nervous system stimulant. To avoid these effects, other drugs are used. A user is freebasing; it's 2 A.M. He must get up at 6 A.M. to make a 7 A.M. job. He can't sleep without using a central nervous system depressant. If he uses a depressant he will wake up fatigued. These are some of the more common physical problems contributing to the motivational crisis of the cocaine dependent.

Less is known about the organic damage resulting directly from cocaine abuse than about its psychosocial consequences. We believe that, like alcoholism, cocaine addiction involves associated organic damage arising from the abuse of the drug. One site of this damage is within the coronary arteries. These arteries supply blood, rich in oxygen, to the heart muscle itself. Evidence of coronary artery damage has been observed in autopsies of young adults who have died from cocaine overdose. Reports of this in the medical literature describe the coronary arteries of 18- to 21-year-old cocaine addicts as appearing similar to those of 50- or 60-year-olds. Normally, these blood vessels should be very open and clear, but cocaine causes protracted vasoconstrictions which may damage the blood vessels themselves. The internal lining of the coronary arteries, called intima or smooth muscle, proliferates—expands in size—and basically starts to shut off the passageway within the artery, thereby blocking the essential supply of oxygen-laden blood to the heart.

Another site where physical damage may occur is the brain itself. One particular brain function which is being looked at carefully is serotonin production. In conducting research with some of the amphetamine breakdown products that are pharmacologically related to cocaine, for example, the designer drugs–amphetamine analogs–like MDA and MDMA (ecstasy)–some destruction of key serotonin areas in the brain has been observed.

These serotonin areas affect sleep, and to some degree, mood. I have observed sleep problems among addicts in early recovery to a degree serious enough for me to explore the usefulness of tryptophan, a precursor of serotonin, as a dietary supplement for clients. There is no research on this that I am aware of, however. On the other hand, there are scientific studies of antisocial personality types–those involving volatile, impulsive behavior–which point to low serotonin levels in the brain. Much of this remains speculative, so as a daily practitioner, I am anxious to see further research in this area. Everyday I see problems of impulsive behavior, cravings, and the inability to regulate sleep properly. To many counselors and therapists this may sound like a formula for relapse, but it is the norm among recovering cocaine addicts, and increases to an even higher level, the need for professional treatment.

Another organic problem of great concern is the possibility of chronic obstructive lung disease–what we commonly call emphysema. Freebasing involves inhaling, directly into the bronchial tubes and lungs, a gas that may be 200+ degrees Fahrenheit. The mucosa of the lungs is unprepared to handle that intensity of heat and as a result, we're going to see some early onset emphysema in some of our freebase population, our young adults and adolescents. You will see evidence of damage if you observe the coughing of a heavy freebase user. He is likely to cough up a blackish, bloody-looking sputum.

The continued use of most drugs leads to feelings of depression and anxiety. We know from research literature on alcohol that a person who drinks in a bar becomes more depressed as he continues to drink through the evening.

Depression is often a result of changes in biochemistry brought on by drug use. People who use cocaine deplete the stimulating neurotransmitters in their brains–such as dopamine. (A characteristic of Parkinson's Disease is low levels of dopamine.) When people have low dopamine levels they typically feel depressed. They do not experience joy. The symptom is called anhedonia, from the word hedonism, meaning pursuit of joy.

Persons who have used cocaine excessively have depleted neurotransmitters in the brain. They feel depressed and remorseful about all the money they've spent. They may even have an agitated depression because the fire is still being stoked in there–but there isn't much left to lift the spirit. So they start feeling depressed, anxious, and irritable.

Paranoia is a phenomenon seen in conjunction with the use of stimulants that you don't see as often with depressant-type drug dependencies. With amphetamines, for example, you can get amphetamine psychoses–amphetamine types of paranoia. These tend to last longer than cocaine paranoia. From what I have seen, if there is no other overt psychiatric problem, paranoia stemming from excessive cocaine use will rapidly subside as the body's cocaine level declines.

The cocaine dependent's paranoia is usually "context appropriate." It is based on dangers inherent in the person's life, but exaggerated. If I fear being busted by the IRS or the Narcs, those are the people who I believe are in my closet. Cocaine addicts always tell stories of sitting at home at two o'clock in the morning. "I hear a car go by and I know it must be the police. So I run to the window to look out. The whole night is a progression of going back and forth to the window, checking the cars that go by to see if it is the police out there, instead of a passerby." The mind goes crazy. It starts to play on those fears, exaggerating them. As soon as you take the drug away, the paranoia usually clears up. You may have occasional signs of it for a few days. Some people talk about having it for a few weeks.

It may seem surprising to hear that this paranoia can actually be converted to a positive force in a treatment program. Low levels of paranoia can become a motivation for recovery if the counselor or therapist is sensitive to this and knows how to handle it. For example, if a client is afraid that someone at work is going to do something bad, it is helpful to talk about all the ways to guard against that happening. "What can you do to keep that supervisor from getting on you? You can always let her know if you have to leave early. You can always take appropriate breaks; come back from lunch on time; show up in the morning on time." A therapist can adjust his or her responses to fit the constellation of fears revealed by each individual client. In essence, a counselor can work with some of the paranoia as long as it does not interfere with a client's ability to undertake required daily activities.

The earliest recovery phase, "control reversal," begins when the denial of the drug problem is pierced and the painful realities of addiction start to break through. The cocaine dependent becomes intensely conscious that there is a problem. The escalation of environmental pressures–social, personal, legal and economic–is a prerequisite to the personal growth stages of treatment.

While becoming dependent on cocaine, the person has developed an elaborate system of defense—especially denial and projections—a beautiful way of minimizing what is going on. As cocaine dependents, they have developed a way of pigeonholing things. They keep one problem in this corner, another problem on the job in another corner, and some other nasty items tucked back somewhere else. Never shall they all meet.

The intensifying psychosocial pressures, however, begin to break down some of this denial and the system begins to falter. We start to see a person who is literally sick. There is no longer any doubt that something is wrong. Yet the therapist, or anyone else trying to help, is still on the receiving end of all the defenses they have built up to avoid the painful reality of addiction.

Inevitably, however, the pain breaks through and precipitates a motivational crisis. When a cocaine dependent reaches this important crossroad, it is necessary to keep the pain level elevated. I don't say, "You are going to be okay," or, "Just hang in there." I believe that trying to find painless ways to change is an unproductive and ineffectual approach to drug addiction therapy. Pain is an important part of the recovery process. Even when a client comes in and says, "My life is worthless; my life is out of control," I look at him and say, "Yes you're right. And some areas may be even worse than you think they are." This sets the stage for keeping the pain level up. It may be the only motivational tool I have to begin with.

Even then, at the height of the motivational crisis, there is ambivalence. Cocaine use remains attractive even after massive losses, and even while in the process of admitting the problem and seeking help. Rarely do cocaine dependents come to a clinic and talk about psychosocial issues and inpatient care. All they may claim to be looking for is relief from the physical complaints. That's why outpatient remedies are most often sought.

Even when in the midst of a crisis, cocaine dependents don't see themselves as "junkies." They see themselves as productive people. This is in direct contrast to many of the stereotypes of drug users. Although cocaine use is pervasive in lower socioeconomic areas, the clients seen in private practice or clinics more often conform to this general profile: 29 year-old female or 30 year-old male; many earning or having earned $25,000 a year or more; spending $500-$700 per week on cocaine.

These people see themselves as still productive, capable of producing income and governing their lives. Moreover, even when they seek treatment, there is a part of them that still wants desperately to use cocaine. That paradox exists in all drug dependents who seek treatment, regardless of the substance of abuse. That paradox is extraordinarily strong in the cocaine addict–protected by control and power urges. The more power and control issues there are, the more difficult it is to motivate the cocaine addict to accept inpatient treatment. To surrender one's independence, even temporarily, is seen as a personal defeat.

Sometimes, extreme measures have been used to try to shock addicts into accepting their addiction. These measures, especially if coercive, rarely work. Often the result is what might be considered a power struggle between the treatment and the patient. When I look at some of the practices designed to help the cocaine dependent regain control, I am critical. I sometimes see coercive strategies being used or recommended that were abandoned fifteen or twenty years ago in the area of alcoholism treatment. The basic trouble with coercive strategies is that even when they seem to work, they are contrary to the psychological principles of acceptance of the addiction, and more consistent with the willpower model, long since proven unsuccessful.

A technique that is described in the professional literature on addiction therapy is called contingency contracting. The greatest contingency contractor was Ben Franklin. Ben was involved in doing some of the early work on the frontier. Once he was building a fort, and the minister came up to him and said, "Ben, I just can't get people to come up and go through my services. What can I do?" Ben said, "No problem!" He suggested that they distribute the rum at the end of each religious service. So from then on the church was packed. If you didn't go to church, you didn't get your portion of rum. In a way, that is a positive approach to conditioning, getting people to do something and then meeting one of their perceived needs. We don't give a cocaine dependent rum, but we can use other rewards.

Contingency contracting, as practiced in drug therapy, usually includes an aversive consequence. You monitor a person's urine to determine if he has been using. If he has been using drugs, some undesirable but agreed-to event, outlined in a preexisting contract, occurs. In one example, a C.P.A. agrees to write a letter to his accreditation board stating:

> *Dear Chairperson,*
> *I am a cocaine addict and my life is totally out of control. I urge you to revoke my license to practice as a C.P.A in this state.*

This letter is given to the therapist. He holds it over the client's head. If the client happens to relapse, the letter is sent to the certification board.

I believe contingency contracts of this type should be used only as a last resort. What I prefer is a more positive approach to the modification of behaviors: positive instead of negative contingencies. I find my clients respond well to goals and direction. So I try to turn the whole contracting process around. I begin by establishing simple goals, and reward their completion. I like that approach because it builds an ability to delay gratification. This is a skill that is underdeveloped in many cocaine dependent people. I always try to understand the reward system of each cocaine dependent. For some it is money. For others it may be position or family.

Life Stabilization Management

In Chapter 3 I talked about finding the big picture by doing a "Columbo-type" technique. Besides an alcohol and drug history, I do a thorough psychosocial assessment and then merge the two, looking for problems and patterns. When I combine a client's psychosocial history with his alcohol and drug history, a more revealing picture of the chemical dependency problem emerges than from either technique alone. Neither of these information gathering activities is just a paperwork exercises. They both provide essential facts for planning a recovery program.

When I do a psychosocial assessment I don't like to bring up the results of the alcohol-drug assessment. I don't ask, "How much did you drink and how much did you drug when you were going through the first divorce?" These questions are guaranteed to trigger defensive reactions. Once a client is stabilized, I try to do an alcohol-drug assessment involving self-ratings in reaction to highly specific questions like: "When was your first use of co- caine? How much did you use in your early twenties and early thirties?" I start building a chronological picture of drug and alcohol use. Comparing this with the psychosocial history captures the chronology, the historical development of problems. By collapsing the two, I can start to break down some of the pigeonholing of different types of problems that is so common among cocaine dependents.

This is the big picture. When the therapist and the client talk about these facts, the client begins to see the cause and effect relationship between the use of cocaine and other drugs and the psychosocial problems involving job, family, and the law. I find it best to wait a few days between doing the drug-alcohol assessment and the psychosocial assessment. Typically, I have clients sketch their own psychosocial histories, as an assignment. I ask them to do it in their own room at night, if they are in a residential program, and then bring it in and talk about it the next day.

I also do a life stabilization/management process with every client who has reached the crisis stage. It provides a foundation for all the therapy that is done later. It involves getting an accurate picture of the client's lifestyle and drugs of choice. Later, I talk about why people make the choices they do, and work toward stabilizing and maintaining his or her life.

At the crisis stage, the cocaine addict's desire to use willpower and control to "conquer" the addiction is a threat to recovery. In order to deal with this problem effectively we must be sensitive to its origins. I have become convinced that the key to acceptance lies in the addict's ability to perceive it in terms he can understand and within a context to which he can relate. It is a matter of conceptual packaging.

In working with a client's acceptance of addiction, I use art therapy, for example, to explore the ideas of powerlessness over cocaine and surrender versus compliance. I have to do everything I can to help bring into the open the addict's perception of what accepting addiction and the unmanageability of life really means. What are the implications of admitting, "My life is out of control."? As an educational approach, my therapy addresses the self. I'm more concerned about the existential aspects of addiction than providing lessons about cocaine the drug and its evils. The latter approach may be appropriate, but as Howard Hughes put it, "for someone else, somewhere else," not here at this crossroads.

Once the treatment program begins, I watch for patients who come in and say things like, "Things just aren't the same as they used to be. I am just not feeling very good today." Maybe something has happened, a subjectively distressing experience that only they are aware of. They can't identify the feeling or where it came from and so they look around and create a crisis. This helps the brain explain what the body is feeling.

One of the most interesting lessons I learned was while working with an alcoholic, about eight years ago. He came to me and said, "I just can't talk to you today because my son is smoking pot." Now, we hear that sometimes. Believing him, I did a wonderful intervention on the family and got the kid into treatment. Dad relapsed.

The dad relapsed because I was so naive at the time that I did not turn that subjective distress back to him and talk to him about what was going on in his life. I "bought" what he told me hook, line and sinker, that the son was the problem. Actually, the son had been smoking pot for ten years. It was never an issue until then. The rule I learned is simple: Whenever you see a recovering person getting out of balance, especially the cocaine dependent, he will start to create excitement. He will create a life crisis.

I am convinced that we must start to work with cocaine dependents during the motivational, or crisis period, implanting the concepts of illness, acceptance, and surrender. Even the way the counselor words his messages is critically important because there must be a total understanding on the part of the client that he is responsible for, and in control of, his own recovery. Even the way Valium or other prescriptions are introduced should be consistent with this principle of personal responsibility. For example, I never say, " This pill will make you better." I say instead, "This pill will help you manage yourself better."

Beginning with the earliest treatment encounters with the cocaine dependent, a sensitive therapist or counselor searches for clues about what is going on inside the addict that will enable him to see himself as chemically dependent, and help him become comfortable with that idea. At this stage, I only hope to firmly establish the addiction concept. Consideration of other drugs used, the alcohol and the pot, will occur later. So, right from the start, getting the concept of addiction implanted and trying to get the cocaine dependent into the appropriate level of care is essential in creating a foundation for recovery.

Always remember that the cocaine dependent has two different people sitting on his shoulder. These represent conflicting feelings. One is saying, "Get the hell out of here." And then there is that strong side that says, "You're in the right place." A basic treatment challenge is to find the leverage you need to keep a person in treatment, when the weak side rears its ugly head and says, "Get the hell out of here because you know what would make you feel better." The next chapter will consider how early treatment encounters help maintain the commitment needed to insure continuous progress toward recovery.

Chapter 5

EARLY TREATMENT ENCOUNTERS

Detoxification is usually the first step in cocaine dependency treatment. Detoxification involves the client's withdrawal from an intoxicating substance with the least possibility of physical injury and minimal physical and psychological discomfort. Cocaine detoxification requires careful, professional management, especially when it is accompanied by central nervous system depressant withdrawal arising from polydrug abuse. Although toxicity can, with time, subside on its own, the client should be in a supervised setting where competent medical care is immediately available in the event of a medical crisis. Chemical restraints may also be required to treat the patient humanely and to prevent self-inflicted injuries.

Since cocaine is an addictive substance, withdrawal from it produces a consistent and readily observable set of behaviors. A person in withdrawal from cocaine looks almost, at times, like someone a little stuporous from taking too many central nervous system depressants. Often we see considerable confusion and, initially, dysphoria

—feeling bad. Then, after twenty-four to forty-eight hours, we begin to see profound depression, often accompanied by headaches, irritability and sleep disturbances.

Let's consider someone who is freebasing one thousand dollars worth of cocaine per week. Our first concern is detoxification and dealing with the behavioral correlates of toxicity and withdrawal. Some cocaine users require detoxification but don't want to enter inpatient treatment because they see it as too restrictive. They may also be poor candidates for, or resist continuing, outpatient treatment. One thing is almost certain, though. Detoxification alone isn't a treatment solution for people who are compromised by chronic cocaine addiction. Intake into a carefully structured treatment program should follow the crisis.

Toxicity

A prime indicator of toxicity is agitation. The person just cannot remain still. Instead of the psychomotor retardation characteristic of alcoholic intoxication, cocaine users are "all over the place." They show some grandiosity, elation, and they tend to talk a lot. They are distractible. Their auditory acuity appears heightened. They hear sounds that other people do not hear and may react to them with fear and paranoia. I described this hypervigilance as a "Ping Pong match" phenomenon. Hypervigilance is often followed by paranoia that, as I have said, is context-appropriate.

Mild to moderate symptoms of cocaine overdose are often ignored by cocaine users and so the cases which come to the attention of a clinic are the more severe ones. A point is reached where, after snorting, freebasing or injecting for a considerable period of time, cocaine's effects become the reverse of the euphoria originally sought and experienced. I have heard addicts say, "I get this strange, funny feeling at times, this general feeling of malaise. Sometimes I can just keep snorting or freebasing and I can work my way through it."

Another manifestation of moderate cocaine overdose is profuse perspiration. I saw a fellow perspire so profusely that you could watch the sweat bead up on his toes and fingers. The sweat would just drip and run. This is not always from a massive overdose, but from a moderate overdose. I remember sitting in an airport in 1971 and breaking out in a sweat. In less than five minutes the sweat was dripping off me. I sneaked off to the bathroom every fifteen minutes while waiting for the plane. I reached a point where I had moderate symptoms of cocaine overdose. I remember watching all the people watching me. I tried to explain to them that I had the flu.

Clients who are concerned about the possibility of having developed an addictive pattern of cocaine use should be asked about reverse effects and sweating because they are mild symptoms of overdose. This is not the full-blown toxic episode, however. You see more profound types of problems with cocaine when you get into the higher dose levels—especially with freebasers and I.V.-users. High-dose users sometimes report pseudo-hallucinations such as "snow lights," flecks of white or silver light in the peripheral vision field.

There are some very serious toxic complications from cocaine overdose, especially the disruption of the body's temperature regulation. A person who is using too much cocaine can die from elevated body temperature. The body temperature can reach 107 or 108 degrees and stay there. This condition is called hyperpyrexia. Treatment for hyperpyrexia involves providing life support systems and body cooling. Thorazine is sometimes used to block some of the heat build up. But, if a person is prone to seizure, Thorazine can be dangerous because it lowers the seizure threshold. A person taking Thorazine can enter into "status epilepticus," repeated grand mal seizures. When you start to get into status epilepticus, you don't get enough oxygen to your brain. Severe brain damage can result.

In cocaine psychosis, many people hallucinate. As long as a treatment professional is in control, this isn't a problem. There are many variations of the bizarre. I can remember talking to a relative who wasn't there. Another time, I remember a friend of mine reporting the actual conversation he had with another friend. That friend was one hundred miles away, but the conversation was so vivid and clear it seemed real. Many patients tell me they love to reach a point where they start to hallucinate. They enjoy that aspect. It doesn't trouble them.

Another symptom of cocaine psychosis is seeing "cocaine bugs." The bugs may appear to be anywhere in the room, even on the person's skin. One client brought a piece of his own flesh in a vial, so he could convince a medical doctor that there actually were cocaine bugs under his skin. This phenomenon is similar to delirium tremens (D.T.s) seen in the withdrawing alcoholic.

In an area such as San Francisco, where there are few treatment beds, cocaine psychosis is sometimes treated on an outpatient basis. They often administer Haldol several times a day, and bring addicts in for counseling–just for reality grounding. Psychotic behaviors are usually transient.

We must always consider the possibility of other drugs complicating detoxification because cocaine addicts often have a history of medicating themselves. Earlier I mentioned the use of heroin and opiates to treat cocaine psychosis and other psychoses. Cocaine dependent clients use this "street cure." Pot, alcohol, Valium or any of the opiates, especially heroin, help them deal with some of the side effects of cocaine toxicity. As the cocaine starts to clear from the blood the toxicity will clear up. About the only time intervention is essential is when a client completely loses contact with reality. If you look into his eyes, and there's "no one home," or there's "someone else at the wheel," he is having a psychotic episode. Episodes of this depth mandate a structured, inpatient clinical environment.

The paranoid-schizophrenic presentation is one in which we see a lot of violent, crazy, acting out behavior. It is not, however, a widely encountered phenomenon in treatment and certainly not a central characteristic of cocaine addiction or withdrawal, as implied by the media's selective reporting. The paranoid part of paranoid-schizophrenic implies an intense feeling that someone is out to get you or harm you, to do something bad to you. The schizophrenic part is a thought process disorder. A thumbnail sketch of the paranoid-schizophrenic would be someone whose thoughts are confused or "crazy" and who is afraid that folks are out to get him.

The real danger occurs when this form of toxicity is acted on. An addict looks at someone and thinks, "Gees, I know that person has a gun. He's probably going to shoot me. So I pull my rod out and blast him before he has a chance to get me." We see this in domestic situations where a husband or wife will accuse the other partner of infidelity. The outcome can be extremely violent.

In an inpatient environment, there seem to be certain times when the cocaine addict has most difficulty and may act out. As with just about every drug, there are some immediate behavioral consequences of withdrawal, and later on some acting out may arise. This is not well-documented in the clinical journals but I have consistently observed it. Often, between days seven and fourteen of treatment, there is a secondary phenomenon that is not the acute abstinence syndrome of early withdrawal. I call it "overamping." It's similar to a free-floating anxiety, but clients often can't put their fingers on what's behind it. This "overamping" causes them to have difficulty participating in group therapy and education programs. They may violate some of the program rules and this, in turn, may put them in a position where other patients and staff members confront them. Typically this secondary reaction subsides in about ten days.

Several different medications are used in treating the symptoms of cocaine withdrawal. For example, if the person has an agitated depression with difficulty sleeping, Valium may be prescribed by the attending physician. The medications most used to deal with the discomfort of early withdrawal are the benzodiazepines–Valium and Librium, among others.

Treating cocaine withdrawal symptoms with medication is complicated by the client's possible abuse of a central nervous system depressant, such as alcohol or Valium, or any tranquilizing or sleep medications, along with the cocaine itself. A person who is already on high doses of Valium must be slowly weaned from that. For the person going through withdrawal from alcohol or the benzodiazepines–Valium and Librium–and the barbiturates, there is the possibility of violent seizures or a slowing of the emerging profile of withdrawal.

In the case of the benzodiazepines, withdrawal is delayed because these drugs have a very long half-life. We know Valium, for example, is fat-soluble. This enables it to remain in the system after the cessation of heavy use until it is gradually metabolized. If there is a fear that a client in cocaine treatment will experience alcohol or other depressant withdrawal, he is often given a prophylactic medication for several days–some drug with a longer half life.

During withdrawal from cocaine, tricyclic antidepressants are used also. Theoretically, these drugs increase the level of norepinephrine in the brain. They ease the depression and drug craving that may be associated with detoxification. There are reports that excessive sleeping during withdrawal (hypersomnia or lethargy) is corrected by tricyclic antidepressants. Lithium has been researched, too. Sometimes Tyrosine and Tryptophan are used, both naturally occurring amino acids. They are the precursors of stimulatory neurotransmitters, dopamine, serotonin, and norepinephrine, depleted during cocaine use.

My real concern, especially if considerable anguish is involved and there is any past history of self-destructive behavior, is that the person withdrawing from cocaine be monitored closely. A potential for self-destructive behavior exists.

It is difficult to type the cocaine addict in terms of early treatment characteristics. Each client presents a unique mix of drug-use, behavioral, emotional, motivational, and family characteristics. However, I would like to describe two kinds of backgrounds which I encounter so frequently that it may be appropriate to refer to them as "types" of clients. The first is the chronic drug abuser of a variety of drugs, often depressants, who eventually discovers cocaine and becomes addicted. The second type is the controlled binge drug-user who discovers cocaine and enters a new, compelling, and intense addictive pattern.

The first type, the chronic drug abuser, has a lengthy history of using alcohol and perhaps opiates. There may be a DUI in his history. He may have been previously treated for a drug dependency. Six months, a year, two years ago, he discovered cocaine. As a friend of mine, Dan Angres, describes cocaine, "It's the great precipitator." Because it's so progressive, cocaine just "blows you right out of the water." Even if this type of client has not been treated for his depressant addictions, he probably has a long history of abuse. Given another three, four, or five years without cocaine, they would probably have entered treatment for Valium, alcohol or opiate problems. Instead, cocaine became "the great precipitator."

The chronic drug abuser who has become addicted to cocaine often displays the characteristic facade of the cocaine addict in early treatment encounters, but after a week or two begins to seem more like the alcoholic who also smokes pot and does downers. He displays intense and varied forms of denial. His family will also have developed an elaborate denial system from years of covering up for the past abuse. This client will not be amenable to hearing, "Cut that crap out. Don't you see you're like an alcoholic?" No, he doesn't. His denial is the disavowal of painful reality. It doesn't exist. During his motivational crisis, the denial started to break down and the pain began to set in. This was often precipitated by a family member, magistrate, or employer putting the pressure on. The result is that this cocaine addict will look a lot like other drug abusers seen by drug counselors.

More frequently, however, I'm seeing a second and more unfamiliar type of addictive pattern. This is the person who may have experimented with alcohol, maybe a little LSD, has never had treatment or a DUI, has probably had some abusive episodes, but often he will tell you these were planned. He would have said, "Yeah, Saturday there's a wedding reception. I'm going to go out and I'm going to get loaded because that's what we do." Very little loss of controlled behavior appears in the case history unless it was premeditated. This is not a person we would typically expect to see in a residential or hospital-based treatment program, but on rare occasions we may see one coming through the court systems for DUI's and other legal problems. But anywhere from a year to four years ago, maybe two to six months if he is an adolescent, he discovered cocaine and fell in love with the drug.

In early treatment, this person is going to look just like the first type I described because the biochemistry is the same. But after the toxicity starts to clear, what emerges is quite different, especially in the area of family involvement. I encounter a lot of projection here as the preferred psychological defense. The family is in deep shock, without the presence of denial . . . just in shock. Sometimes this shock is so profound that the family members seem like they're trauma victims.

Program Intake

I have found that any isolation of the client during this early treatment period tends to promote leaving the treatment program. When people in pain are isolated, they make the worst case out of everything. If you are waiting for your boy friend or girl friend, and he or she is thirty minutes late, what do you tend to do if you are sitting there by yourself? You probably play worst case, looking for all the bad outcomes that might happen. Similarly, strong impulses to leave treatment can be a direct result of the patient's having been left alone to build worst cases.

If I have a cocaine addict I'm bringing through the intake process, and I say, "Go sit in room 167 and the nurse will be in to take care of you," it may take fifteen to twenty minutes for the nurse to get there. By that time, I may have someone profoundly emotional and scared, who has built himself to a point where he's ready to walk out of the treatment program. This is why the best way to work with addicts on an inpatient basis involves the direct transfer of care, from the direct supervision of one staff member to another.

It is never easy to get the cocaine addict to recognize the need for inpatient treatment. For one thing, we are dealing with the control needs of the individual. If this is the case, there's not much that can be done besides keeping the pain level up, trying to keep the family from enabling, establishing a concept of addiction, and starting to move toward the goal of in-depth acceptance.

As soon as possible, I try to gain as much factual information as I can about the cocaine client's addictive pattern. Where is the client located in overall progression? Knowing certain key facts helps me work more effectively with the critical area of addiction acceptance. I look for evidence of increased tolerance, that a person has really escalated his dosage, and the loss of behavior control. I approach the loss of control indirectly, asking something like, "Look, how many times did you buy cocaine from your dealer early in the week even though you didn't want to use it until the weekend, figuring that if you waited till later he would cut it up? And how often were you able to do a few lines and put the rest away for the weekend? How often was it all used up before the weekend?" This is a way of getting at the loss of controlled behavior, similar to that of the alcoholic.

Having the right person available at intake can make the difference between an addict starting a successful recovery program, or backing away. In directing clinical programs I have always made it a policy to identify the staff members who are most effective at assessment-intake because it is a job which demands exceptional sensitivity and interpersonal skill. The best intake counselors I know could probably sell cars like crazy, because here they face the challenge of convincing an addict that this program, which he doesn't really know much about, will help him control himself during a tough period of time.

During the first few days after an addict steps in the door I try to "get to where the client is," as quickly as possible. At the same time, the addict needs to be convinced that appropriate treatment is available for him and that he will get better. Establishing rapport with the cocaine addict who just walked in the door is a challenge because he will often use a presentation of specialness and uniqueness to emotionally distance himself from me. Although he's desperately trying to say he's different, he has one big thing in common with everyone else seeking treatment for an addiction to alcohol or any other drug: he's scared.

Presenting one's self as an extraordinary person is a form of self-defense, a means of keeping others at a safe emotional distance. People who have worked with alcoholics notice the difference in initial presentation of self. Alcoholics will often demonstrate excessive compliance. The cocaine addict is a little more "up front" to begin with. At least you can clearly see and feel what you are dealing with.

To cocaine dependents the appeal of specialness is incredible, even though they are chemically addicted just like so many others. Knowing this, you can sometimes come up with ways to turn an exaggerated sense of specialness into something positive for recovery. If the sense of specialness is all the client will give me to work with, I use it however I can to help him.

In responding to this presentation of specialness, it's important for me to not let it control my own reactions. I try to not let myself become angry and adversative. For example, I often hear the cocaine addict say, "Cocaine is the only thing that I've ever lost control over, so don't tell me I have to quit smoking dope." As a therapist I have a choice. I can sit there and get angry, tell him, "You're just like any alcoholic," or "You're just a junkie," or "Cut that crap out." I can escalate a power struggle, but if I do, I'm playing his game in his court. He's in my backyard now, but instead I'd be feeding into his control system. Instead of finding out where he is and what his perceptions are, I'd be attacking his beliefs. With a client who is prone to projection, who's not going to deal too well with confrontation, who's also using a drug that causes paranoia and is very illegal, this approach doesn't lead to good self-disclosure.

Instead, I smile inside and say, "Look, I have a treatment program tailored just for you that is going to work. I have the right milieu, special therapy groups–women's groups, Vietnam Vets groups, sexual abuse groups, special assignments and a special program. I have a special approach for building self-help skills. I have a world of tools and ample time to use them." By taking this approach I can work with the "specialness," and as a result, fewer addicts voluntarily terminate their treatment program. Using this approach allows me to establish rapport and to find out how the client thinks and feels.

To knock out some of the uncertainty I give new clients tours, taking them to the dayroom, linking them up with other patients. I ask focused questions like, "Where would you like to do your paperwork?" "Where would you like to fill out this form?" "Would you like to do it in your room? Would you like to do it in the dayroom? Or, would you like to do it right here at the desk and I'll get you a cup of decaf?" By using this approach, our goals coincide. I need the form filled out; the client chooses where he's going to do that, which gives him a sense of control.

Sometimes I make leading comments that appeal to that sense of specialness. I know that when I start to work with a cocaine addict, I have two tasks. One task is to create some structure in his life. The second is to provide some initiative. The structure is the treatment program. How can I draw that person in and keep him coming back to a recovery program?

One approach I have used successfully goes like this. A person with a cocaine problem comes in to ask about treatment. I say, "Yes, the person who referred you called me and told me about you. She told me you were very special, and that you move quite quickly. I only take people who move quickly." If you want to see a glow on someone's face, watch the cocaine addict when you say this.

I am reminded of a very beautiful, twenty-eight-year-old woman. I was sitting there talking to her. She had been on the unit about twelve hours and was going through the confusion and dysphoria that accompanies cocaine withdrawal. She had a three thousand dollar-a-week habit and had been prostituting herself from drug dealer to drug dealer to support it. She was sitting there, bent over, weeping and looking at me with her mascara running. A fifty-year-old alcoholic walks through the door and this lady pulls herself up, stands up and says, "I do three thousand dollars of cocaine a week. What do you do?" This is a self-perception of specialness.

Once I get through that first couple of weeks, I may need to become adversative at some point. This may be in response to the same leitmotif: variations on this theme of specialness. Some illustrations are: the client who works other peoples programs but not his own; the client who advises you about how to run your unit; the client who tells everyone else how to get better. I've had patients who will patronize or look down on alcoholics–"They're just using alcohol; I'm using cocaine." Then, too, there is the formation of little cliques that start to do things in the unit that aren't very therapeutic. But I won't let myself become adversative until I have built a solid relationship of trust and rapport with a client.

If a special cocaine treatment unit is available, it goes a long way toward selling the cocaine dependent on inpatient treatment. A unit of this type conveys an image of uniqueness. A special unit to meet the needs of the cocaine dependent has proven to be economically feasible in larger hospitals or multiple treatment facilities. Such units are quickly filled and have waiting lists. However, they must provide basic chemical dependency services to be successful.

In an inpatient environment there is structure. We have therapeutic settings, self-help meetings, structured time. We can organize this administratively, but initiative is the part we must create in our interaction with the clients. Providing structure and taking the initiative means dealing with the specialness, getting them involved, and bringing them to see themselves as part of the unit, not as an extra cog. Once they begin to see this happen, as they start to work in the milieu, in meetings and self-help groups, they start to develop a sense of hope. They see people who are like them, with the same problems, doing better. If we start working with the initiative, dealing with the specialness, going ahead and playing with that narcissistic child inside, we will have better luck at "keeping them in the ball game."

When I have clients coming in, seeing themselves as special–but not belonging–one of the things I try to do is to "get them hooked into" other cocaine people. This way they can know, "We are not alone. We're not the only people who have this problem." This is how I start the process of identification.

I take the patients into the day room, into the milieu, and introduce them to at least two or three other cocaine or polydrug addicted persons. I try to get them to start telling drug-a-logues. That is their common denominator at this point. Hope arises from knowing a problem is not unique, when others share their problems and aspirations for recovery.

If I am involved with intake, the first thing I do is work with the concept of addiction. While trying to keep the pain level up, I take the patient and directly introduce him to the nurse who would be doing the physical nursing assessment. As I mentioned earlier, I think that is crucial, a good transfer of care. The nurse does her assessment, then introduces the patient to the technician or a counselor-assistant who can do the belonging search.

Next, I introduce the primary counselor, so we can start to lay the groundwork and get this person involved. I say to the cocaine dependent, "There is a part of you that wants to leave, isn't there?" (And you know this is a big part of him, at this early stage.) "There is also a part of you that brought you in here, and knows what is best for you. Is that not so? I want to congratulate you on that strong side of you, because only ten to fifteen percent of the cocaine dependents have the guts to come in and face their problem." Again, I appeal to that specialness. I say, "You are special. You are one of the few people who has the guts to come and do what you are doing. When that ugly part of you rears its ugly head, I want you to contract to sit down and talk to me before making any decisions."

The Outpatient Option

A key question in treating the cocaine addict is: "Should this client receive an inpatient or an outpatient program?" To complicate matters, the answer to this question isn't always derived from a consideration of what's best for the addict. Wealthy clients have all the options available to choose from; the poor, a few or none. What should ideally be a medical and psychosocial decision is, in reality, permeated with political and financial considerations.

The "cocaine epidemic," changes in the economics of healthcare, and sociopolitical factors have forced us to examine, more closely than ever before, the outpatient treatment option. To be specific, large corporations, whose medical benefit programs have paid for intensive inpatient care for addicted employees, are beginning to demand more cost-effective treatments for a growing number of employees. Some of the major medical insurance providers are moving in this direction, too. One outcome is that treatment programs will be required to articulate clear and precise criteria for admission to a program, assignment to a treatment type (outpatient or inpatient), and standards for release. Relapse monitoring procedures will become more widespread.

Are there universal criteria for judging whether an individual should enter an outpatient, as opposed to an inpatient, treatment program? What about the possibility of outpatient treatment for someone who has lost control of his behavior through dependency, but still has a healthy family? A cocaine dependent says he is willing to enter

Alcoholics Anonymous and Cocaine Anonymous, and is willing to work through weekly outpatient counseling. Is he doomed to fail? Possibly. The issues are complex.

We've been able to show in studies that cocaine addiction treatment is effective, but we can't precisely forecast which treatment format, outpatient or inpatient, will guarantee a better outcome for a given individual client. We can make some reasoned judgments based on our professional observations and past experiences, but there remains room for error.

I think that high dose users, especially freebasers and people who are injecting intravenously, are going to need inpatient care. The reason is that this addict will undoubtedly have the biochemical alterations and severe environmental traumas that accompany high dose use. These complications are extremely difficult to treat in an outpatient program. Also, high dose cocaine users will typically be polydrug abusers. These are indicators for inpatient care. And what about life-threatening withdrawal and medical or psychiatric problems? A person displaying a psychotic episode generally needs inpatient stabilization.

At the psychosocial level, we must consider what's at stake for the client. What does he have to lose if our placement is wrong? Does he have too much at risk to put him in a basic outpatient program where he is seen once or twice a week–his family, his job? Will the family cooperate and support the treatment program? Were there previous episodes of outpatient failure with a disease that's now progressed further? If so, the client is worse off this time than he was before and, in addition, has a track record of failure.

Old friends can bring you down. A cocaine addict in an outpatient program usually has no healthy subset of friends. The people he will associate with are the same as before he entered treatment. A problem I run into if I put a person back into an unhealthy social setting is that these friends are likely to have a vested interest in undermining the recovery program. Friends of the recovering cocaine dependent too often use this faulty logic: "I run with you all the time and you and I don't have a problem. All of a sudden you say to yourself, 'I have a problem,' and go into treatment. What does that say about me? I have to do some self-evaluation. What am I going to do the next time you come around? If you are doing well, and we used to run together, and now you say that you have a problem, I'm going to try to pull you down to my level. Then neither of us has a problem. When I have to introspect myself and evaluate myself based on you, and you are doing well, that makes me feel bad."

Clearly, practicing how to relate to drug-using friends must receive priority attention in a treatment program. I often do this by surprise. I will have a person sit there and I'll just get up in his face and say, "You know I am a friend of yours. You know I have been with you for fifteen years and we have drugged for a long time. Who the hell are those people in the treatment center anyway? They have only known you for ten, fifteen, twenty days. Tell me about those pussies. Come on, we've been out on the street a long time. Come on, let's do a couple of lines." Verbally, he has no response because he's distraught by emotion. The intellect "goes right down the tubes." He can sit there and tell you, "What I would like to do is tell these people that if I'm really their friends they'd accept my addiction and support me." But I have to get in his face and let him practice saying it. He must be comfortable with those statements—or in a real confrontation he will lose his good intentions.

When arranging outpatient treatment, I develop a contract with the client which states that if the outpatient approach fails he will enter inpatient treatment. And what is meant by failure must be clearly defined. To do this I ask concrete questions like, "What does it mean for you to be out of control? What must happen for you to be able to see yourself as out of control?" The client may say that he can't get up and go to work anymore, or "I don't have money to pay the bills." Clients must start to establish some way that, when they relapse on an outpatient basis, they can start to see themselves as part of a progressive model of addiction.

I have had good results with a large number of snorters, and a few freebasers and injectors, seeing them two to three times a week for the first two to three months, on an outpatient basis. I have done that with people who have no history of attempted suicide nor of repeated failure on an outpatient basis. They should have some family support, although the family may be in denial or shock, experiencing some difficulty. There should be a willingness to become involved in Alcoholics Anonymous and Cocaine or Narcotics Anonymous, and no more than mild to moderate impairment in thought and emotional processes. If someone is grossly impaired in thinking and feeling, you cannot work with that person in an outpatient environment.

The SIPIO Option
(Shortened Inpatient/Intensive Outpatient)

We should be aware that motivation is likely to be external in an inpatient treatment program. Also, clients will experience difficulties integrating with the inpatient environment. For these reasons alone, intensive outpatient programming is an attractive concept. I recommend that an effective alternative would combine the best of inpatient and outpatient approaches.

Begin the treatment program with a shortened inpatient stay, seven to fourteen days. During this inpatient period, undertake detoxification and assess the client for self-destructive behavior. I assess the environment and the family, stabilize the person, and begin some self-help work. Then it may be possible to put him into a more intensive outpatient environment, followed by basic continuing care counseling. This approach makes sense and may be the most cost-effective.

We have already begun to see shortened inpatient stays. This will become more prevalent as drug dependency treatment becomes a greater financial burden in the "private pay sector." It is on the way. In working with General Motors, I have seen their length of stay already fall two or three days. In the last year we have started to see more people exposed to intensive outpatient programming, but the programming must involve the family. It also must be aided by self-help, or generally it will not work.

Whatever treatment option is selected, the early encounters are the most significant in setting the stage for a successful recovery program. During toxicity and detoxification, the safety of the user requires knowledgeable guidance. At the same time, a well-executed program intake will facilitate both program planning by the therapist and program acceptance by the addict. At this time, the addict's commitment to recovery must be established, maintained and strengthened. It is not a time to be taken lightly or sacrificed to expediency. Careful, systematic assessment will pay dividends as recovery progresses.

Chapter 6

ACCEPTANCE IN DEPTH

A recovery program is demanding. What it boils down to is asking people to change everything, and to do it quickly. When we make this demand and psychological defense systems remain active, problems will certainly follow. People begin looking around, not seeing themselves as ill with cocaine addiction, looking for excuses and external reasons why they're who and where they are. If this happens, can we expect them to follow through on all our beautiful treatment plans? No. The key to recovery is accepting that a problem exists and moving on from there!

An important challenge for the counselor is to help restructure a client's ideas and assumptions, about the role of willpower and impulse control in addiction, into more workable and highly-personalized concepts. A counselor tries to get the cocaine dependent to accept his powerlessness over the chemical and to become willing to ask for and accept help from another person or group. Once this is achieved, the other parts of the program will fall into place. Without it, there is no consistent program. Only after a person accepts the reality of dependency will we begin to see profound changes in behaviors and attitudes. Once powerlessness is accepted, the individual's energy becomes redirected toward making positive changes instead of defending the status quo.

Acceptance issues vary in form and intensity according to the type of addiction being treated. Consider adult children of alcoholics. They feel their lives are out of control anyway, and they have no problem with the first step of the Twelve Step Recovery program: admitting to powerlessness over life–its fundamental unmanageability. From them we hear, "What do you mean powerless? I'm hopeless." Cocaine addicts have the opposite orientation; they have extreme difficulty letting go and letting things happen. To them, being involved in making something happen is the way to cope with life.

Control and power urges cause cocaine addicts to resist asking for help and these urges reinforce their denial. As I mentioned earlier, a cocaine addict will frequently use projection as a tactic for avoiding acceptance of addiction and its implied powerlessness. A good illustration of this type of projection is the client who said to me not too long ago, "You know, I just can't believe I got in this position. I can't believe that I'm in this treatment program." He continued talking about himself, saying, "You know, I would have never been here; it's the bank's fault. I was writing bad checks, and they were foolish enough to cash them for me. If they hadn't cashed those checks, I would never have had a problem. Those people at the bank really should work on their act; they don't have it together at all."

Pain is a great motivator of acceptance. It is a direct, personal experience that you can't evade. You can't talk your way out of it. The recovering cocaine addict's pain isn't just physical. It's also psychological, emerging from a heightened awareness of the realities of damaged or destroyed family, social, occupational, legal, and economic statuses. A good counselor tries to insure that these realities retain their high profile in the thinking and feeling of the early recovering cocaine addict. Harry Tiebout, in the early AA literature, said it this way: "When the unconscious forces of defiance and grandiosity actually cease to function effectively, the individual is wide open to reality. He can listen and learn without conflict and fighting back." At the other end of the spectrum, I have found that when the pain level drops there is a strong tendency for the doors to close–the door inward to feelings and consciousness, and the door outward toward healthier, adaptive patterns.

The family, often a focal point of the psychological pain reaction of the cocaine addict, has a profound effect on his acceptance of his addiction. Often the families themselves require counseling to cope with what may have appeared as an unexpected crisis. Some families appear to be in deep shock from learning of the cocaine addiction of a loved one. I've had people come in and say, "Gees, I didn't realize he was even using until I looked at the bank account, and all of our money was gone and we couldn't pay the mortgage. I knew he was using a little bit, but I didn't know it had gotten this far out of hand." Then, suddenly, that person left them . . . went out, maybe drug dealing . . . lost his job. A family in shock needs massive initial support and a chance to ventilate. They need reassurance. Denial will not be evident because there just hasn't been time for them to develop an elaborate defense system. The addiction arose too fast for this to happen.

Families with more than a single member involved with cocaine present special problems. These families may actually try to sabotage the addict's treatment program. They may try to prevent an addict from following though on a treatment program because his recovery would pose a threat to their lifestyle. I met a lady in Cincinnati not long ago who told me this story. She said, "You know, I just went through treatment for cocaine addiction. I never realized that I was addicted to the lifestyle and to the drug and that there were anchors in our relationship that very much involved cocaine. When my husband came home from his first cocaine treatment, I came in one night after being out with the girls, a couple of grams in my pocket, acting very seductive. My husband relapsed." She did that twice. Finally, through the intervention of a therapist who got her into treatment, she came to grips with her own problem–the relationship and the way that cocaine was used to create a nice bond, almost a belonging, a sexuality in the couple. The words she used to describe her feelings were, " A life for me without cocaine was like going from Rolex to Timex." She missed the excitement. She missed the drug. And she sabotaged her husband's recovery program.

Another special problem is created by the family involved in the cocaine business. Their involvement in the cocaine business makes it difficult to work with them in a group setting because they may be viewed as perpetrators. One treatment group of chemically dependent families with adolescent children, from an affluent community, completely rejected a family that had been involved in the cocaine business and appeared to take pride in it. This family became the group's scapegoat.

So, all in all, acceptance of addiction is invariably more complicated than it might seem on the surface. Moreover, acceptance of addiction isn't a concrete step, one that we can indisputably prove we're working on or have achieved.

I think that it is best represented as a major internal readjustment. We talk about it in terms of a Higher Power or good modeling. We talk about it in terms of involving a curative factor called "hope." We can look at it in several different ways. Fundamentally, however, it is a conversion process outside the direct, conscious control of either the client or the counselor. Together, we can only create the conditions that maximize the likelihood for acceptance to emerge.

I am still amazed to see people suddenly become comfortable with being addicted. I find this is the same struggle for all chemically dependent persons, although the surface features may appear different from one addiction to another. What is being universally sought is an acceptable answer to the question, "How can I let go and let God?"

In early AA literature, in letters between Bill W. and Carl Jung, Carl talks about the alcoholic and says, "No matter what I did, nothing worked." He said that then "something happened"–at which point he had a conversion reaction or a spiritual conversion–and he became comfortable with his addiction. He was able to maintain a productive lifestyle without returning to drink.

Willpower or Acceptance?

In working with the recovering cocaine addict I am sensitive to both nonverbal and verbal messages which state or imply power urges. These messages often are permutations of two fundamentally different ideas. The first, "willing things to happen," is power-based and foretells continuing difficulties with recovery. In contrast, there is the accepting message of "becoming willing for something to happen." There is a vast psychological gulf separating these two orientations. Using the willpower model implied by the first message, a person says, "I should be able to deal with this problem. I can handle what is going on in my life." Can, should, could, ought –these are all power words. When a person starts to say these things, it's an indicator that he's working a model different from the one that has proven effective in recovery programs.

To create conditions conducive to developing acceptance, I try to engage the client in an awareness-building process. I ask myself again and again, "When does someone become comfortable with the personal awareness of cocaine addiction? Has it happened yet for this client? Does he bang his head against a wall? Does he try to do it his way? Is he like the patient who, after three days, ran out and said, I know exactly what to do now. I make three meetings a week and talk to my wife on Saturday nights. And it's all going to work out. I know exactly what to do now, and know how to control it." That is a flight into hell–a willpower model, and nothing more. Treating chemical dependency with willpower is a recipe for misery. It is very dangerous and it leads to relapse.

One reason that willpower is so inadequate is that self-defeating behaviors, like addictions, seem to have a magnetic attraction. If a person is functioning on willpower alone, putting him in a stressful situation will often trigger the return of the same old self-defeating thoughts and behaviors. You have a person who thinks, "Yes, I need to stay away from this stuff." But his emotions override his intellect. He is going to make some poor judgments. People who operate from a willpower model test their abstinence more than those who accept powerlessness. If you think about it, the implication is: "If I have willpower,

I should be able to test this doggone thing and make it work."

People "running on willpower" put themselves around cocaine. This approach to recovery is sometimes termed "doing it the hard way." They will go right out of the treatment center to a party where they know cocaine will be available. There they become overwhelmed. I often see this self-defeating pattern–attempting recovery the hard way, bargaining away everything helpful.

A patient who is a perfectionist, who is self-critical, and who has the "self-talk" pattern, "Everything I do I must work hard for, or it isn't good," will probably want to test his abstinence by putting himself in a position where cocaine is available, will try to recover the hard way. It's like the alcoholic who wants to go back into the bar and have ginger ale, because he wants to be with friends.

The Power of the Milieu

Outcomes of the acceptance phase aren't totally determined by what happens between the therapist and the patient, or the family-patient-therapist triad. Acceptance begins within the patient and the family but requires interactions with people the client can relate to, identify with, and with whom thoughts and feelings can be openly shared. Patient-to-patient dialogue is therefore crucial to the acceptance process. Acceptance is promoted when one patient is doing well and is modeling something that the other patient would like to have: stability in life.

Why groups? Why are groups the preferred mode of treatment in chemical dependency? Within the therapeutic group all kinds of experiences are recounted. Hidden truths are revealed to others, often for the first time. But most important, ideas and alternatives are explored with critical feedback from others who have been there before. Whatever is being considered, chances are there is someone in the group who has tried that approach four times. And when someone with credibility, someone with genuine first-hand experience, says, "I tried that four times. This is my fifth treatment, and I realize I better change my ways," you have a powerful message. Something constructive happens when a cocaine addict walks into a self-help meeting or treatment group and says, "Yeah, my name is George, and you know, I'm a cocaine addict but, you know, I really don't have trouble with some of those other drugs you guys have problems with, like marijuana and alcohol."

In a residential program, an even more powerful process is at work than in community-based self-help groups because there is continuing and varied involvement with other group members. In a residential program, the addict who makes a statement like the one in the previous paragraph will probably be challenged by someone he was in the dayroom with the night before, someone who ran the same turf and passed him in the night. These patients may have already begun to establish trust, that sense of universality between patients sharing the same problem.

Part of developing acceptance is becoming involved with winners. I try to expose the early recovering cocaine addict to other chemically dependent people who have successfully struggled and dealt with the willpower model. I can often structure a group so that at least one member is like a particular client I'm working with, a member who has worked through acceptance. I encourage them to interact, hoping that growth will occur through modeling.

There are some organizational resources available to both inpatient and outpatient clients that foster acceptance. We have two major organizations for recovering cocaine dependents: Cocaine Anonymous and Narcotics Anonymous. The newer one, Cocaine Anonymous, may require a cautious approach. My fear about Cocaine Anonymous is that there may be times when a recovering addict attends Cocaine Anonymous and the longest period of abstinence represented in the group is only six to nine months. There are no "old timers." The only resources that these novice abstainers may have are the old "drug-a-logues" and "How I used to freebase." There isn't much abstinence value to these. In fact, they may create "cravings" and pressure for relapse.

Sometimes a client will call me after attending a Cocaine Anonymous meetings and say, "What the hell are you doing to me? I got so hungry there, I had to leave." So, whenever possible, I encourage clients to become involved in Alcoholics Anonymous. It is an established organization with a cross-section of members. If there is any alcohol involved in the cocaine dependent's profile, and some willingness to give it up, AA is the modality I always use. However, many AA members do not accept primary cocaine addicts. So, another of my jobs is to find an appropriate and receptive group for the client.

Confronting an addict's lack of acceptance isn't helpful. It doesn't work because it creates an "us against them" atmosphere. Confrontation reinforces the part of every patient that hates the counselor or therapist. Think about it. A person seeks the help of a counselor because some part of his life is out of control. I have yet to meet anyone who likes to be out of control, and even fewer who like to admit it. Instead, the client thinks, "My life is out of control and therefore I need to come to you for help. I am glad you are there, but I am angry that I have to do this to begin with." A successful counselor remains sensitive to the client's need to accept his drug dependency, the recovery process and the counselor's persona. Hard confrontation undermines this.

A good way to foster acceptance of cocaine dependency is through studying written material, especially AA literature. Unfortunately, there is still no established body of self-help material that deals specifically with cocaine dependency and recovery problems. There's a Narcotics Anonymous book available, but no Cocaine Anonymous book.

By carefully assigning readings about addiction and observing a client's reactions to them, I gain information which I can use to help move the recovery process forward. Readings work because the things that jump out at us when we read do so because they are personally significant, meaningful or important. For example, I use some of Tiebout's work as a projective tool. The Tiebout papers are pamphlets that cost about three dollars and fifty cents each. One of them talks about ego factors in early recovery. Another is called *Surrender vs. Compliance*. I give it to the patient as a self-study assignment. The way I frame the assignment is unconventional, though. I don't say, "Read this and tell me what parts apply to you; underline those and we'll talk about it later." I put a different frame around it by saying, "Read this and, whatever interests you, just underline it and bring it in the next time you come. And bring my book back, Okay? Just underline whatever interests you."

What's the difference between asking a client to underline the parts that apply to him, and asking him to underline the parts that interest him? The latter frame will not be as likely to trigger a defensive reaction as the former. This is important because what I want Tiebout's work to be is a projective test. Things will jump out of that pamphlet at the individual for a reason: because they are significant in his own case history.

What will come in is little bits of underlined material that I can start to talk about. This is an opportunity to translate some of the generalized notions into the powerlessness concept. I tie the underlined material into the first step of Cocaine Anonymous or Alcoholics Anonymous, and start to talk in depth about issues such as a Higher Power and the willingness to ask for help.

In closing this chapter I want to emphasize that the foundation built from day one of treatment and the daily personal growth program are both indispensable to recovery from addiction. If the foundation is lacking, or if someone is not working a healthy program, nothing that a therapist does will work right. The recovering cocaine dependent will slide and fall right in front of us. There is no magic to recovery. It's discipline and dedication. It's doing all the little things, daily, that allows one to survive. Recovery is like running down an up-escalator. Stand still and you will lose ground.

Chapter 7

HELPING STRATEGIES

Let's consider a cocaine dependent who has been through a motivational crisis and is working on acceptance. He is attending AA, NA or CA meetings; the family is in treatment; and progress is being shown in what-we-term early recovery. Now the client needs a treatment program which will build the know-how and the strength to live a life without drugs.

Once the client has reached this recovery stage it is premature to say, "You're ready. Now go out and do." A recovering cocaine dependent can't "go out and do" without having first developed the essential strengths and skills that will allow him to handle the high risk situations he will undoubtedly face. Often, at this stage of recovery, the client isn't aware of the cues and anchors that may precipitate a relapse. If my client walks back into his former environment at this stage, I want to be sure he has a repertoire of alternative behaviors to help him deal with some of the issues involved in his addiction. Pushing the limits of a client's weaknesses at this early stage of treatment is a formula for failure. Instead, I try to begin implementing an educational model that speaks directly to the cocaine dependent's unique problems.

Finding a treatment program which is geared to the unique problems of cocaine dependents can be difficult, especially outside the major metropolitan areas. More and more cocaine dependence treatment programs are being offered, but there still aren't enough to meet the mounting needs. One approach is for alcohol treatment centers to make a transition into chemical dependency treatment. Sometimes, however, the expanded alcohol center's educational approach to treating cocaine addiction is based on a chronic alcohol model. If this is the case, there are some things to watch for.

When a treatment program isn't truly geared to meeting the unique recovery needs of the cocaine dependent, the tendency is to try to make the cocaine dependent, a square peg, fit into an alcohol treatment model, a round hole. If a middle-to-chronic alcohol model is followed, one risks reinforcing the idea that the cocaine dependent does not belong in treatment. Most cocaine dependents don't see themselves in a typical portrait of alcoholic problems. They have no liver damage. They have little end organ pathology. Cocaine addiction is a different dynamic and a different progression.

The other problem that alcohol treatment units have in serving cocaine dependents is that their lectures tend to be "Father Martin's Chalk Talks." This is a wonderful movie and I love it. But it isn't meaningful and relevant to the cocaine dependent. You also have dialogues that follow this format: "Let's talk about the progression of alcohol; let's talk about alcoholism, sexuality and recovery. Let's talk about alcoholism and . . . ." This happens because staff members are often recovering alcoholics and the program was developed on the basis of Alcoholics Anonymous.

Sex is another special problem area that must be dealt with differently in a treatment program for the cocaine client. I have found that sexual problems stemming from the use of cocaine often surface during abstinence from the drug. Remember, cocaine may have been a profound aphrodisiac. Sexual problems can be a major source of stress for the client and therefore a threat to his continued recovery. Few alcohol recovery programs emphasize the sexual dimensions of addiction and recovery.

There are special acceptance problems, distinct from those encountered in alcoholism treatment, related to the cocaine addict's use of alcohol and pot as secondary drugs. Some of the return-to-work issues are different for the recovering cocaine dependent than for the alcoholic. We rarely find an alcoholic who owes twenty-five hundred dollars to people on the job. Further, a treatment program's educational model must target the cocaine-related cues and anchors because they are crucial to relapse prevention.

In the cocaine dependency progression, the use of a depressant drug usually occurs before the cocaine dependency becomes predominant. Later, when the cocaine is out of control, so are the earlier depressant drugs—typically marijuana and alcohol. Relapses may follow the same path, from depressant drugs to cocaine. The depressant's key role in the cocaine addict's progression makes it essential to go and look carefully at the escalation of the alcohol and marijuana problems. This is the first helping strategy I mention because the client's unwillingness to abstain from these secondary drugs may prevent him from being accepted in a treatment program for cocaine addiction. And if the patient insists on continuing his use of depressant drugs, there is a high risk that he will also return to cocaine.

I again emphasize that cocaine relapses often tend to start with marijuana and alcohol and then lead back to cocaine. A typical failure in recovery occurs when the client hasn't been convinced of a need to modify his earlier life-style and to abstain from alcohol and pot. He leaves treatment and returns to the same old people, places, and things. He smokes a joint with his friends. They go to a bar, have a beer. Someone say's, "Let's go outside, smoke a joint." They walk out to the parking lot. Someone lights up a joint. Someone else pulls an amber vile out of a pocket . . . then the golden coke spoon.

Suppose a person who has been snorting cocaine, up to three to four hundred dollars per week, comes in to see me about treatment. He wants outpatient treatment but takes the position, "Okay, I'm going to try to give up the cocaine but don't talk to me about giving up the alcohol, and pot. Don't tell me I have to quit drinking. Drinking beer is my God-given right, and no one is going to take that away from me." How do I deal with that?

I have two choices. I can say, "I won't work with you because I only work with people who abstain from all drugs." If I choose that option, I will lose him to any treatment. On the other hand, I can say, "Okay, let's work on the cocaine problem and let's define what 'out of control' means for you, in reference to alcohol and drugs." With this choice, I can keep him in treatment and try to motivate him to take a closer look at his alcohol and pot use. Sometimes I ask the client to prove that he has control over depressant drugs by abstaining from them for three to six months.

As an example of continued depressant use during cocaine dependency treatment, consider the case of a male client, about twenty-nine years old, an aspiring drummer. He was very macho and very handsome. He had used cocaine for two years–all intranasal use. Things were going well until his marriage started to deteriorate. He didn't like some of the things that were going on in his life. His money flow had gotten bad and that had angered his wife. She threatened to leave and he came into treatment.

He came in and said, "Okay, now I want to work on an outpatient basis." I replied, "I am willing, for the first two to three weeks, to see you three times a week. Then we will meet once a week for the next six months." I allowed him to go ahead and continue to drink and to smoke. I did so because my sense was that if I kept him in treatment, at least I had him in a place where I could monitor him. He insisted that cocaine was the only thing that he had ever lost control over. He was a very controlling gentleman and was able to work with the cocaine very nicely.

I also treated him and his wife in couples counseling where I later found out he had slipped and used cocaine one time. It was a one shot instance, about six weeks into his recovery. He convinced himself that he was just chasing an illusion and became a little bit discouraged. He called me up and we talked about it. In some ways it may have been a therapeutic relapse. He learned something from it. In the last seven or eight months he used no cocaine at all. But during the last two months his alcohol consumption escalated.

I talked with him about a progressive model of alcohol use and the typical succession of events. We related it to similar phenomena of his cocaine addiction. Next, we developed a written contract which I linked to daily logs he kept of his activities. His contract stated that he was going to run three or four times a week, make so many meetings, practice drums six times a week, weigh himself every day, and bring the daily records in every time he came to see me. This person, for a while, had no problem at all. He had a couple of beers, a glass of wine in the evening.

Then the alcohol started to progress. He was never "into" pot. I think that in the whole nine months he only smoked a couple of joints. Soon this man, who ran every day and practiced drums, began to skip both. He started to gain weight. He was really "into" looks and became quite disturbed about what was happening to his physique.

One day he came in to see me after being drunk the night before. The first thing that he did was throw up in the bathroom. He came out and said, "I guess it's time to start talking about the alcohol." I sensed that he was at a point where things were ready to fly apart. His wife was concerned about his escalated drinking, that they could not have just one glass of wine. The bottle seemed to magically disappear. They knew there were escalation problems.

His image of his alcohol and marijuana intake predated, by about two years, what he was actually doing at present. We began to spend a lot of time talking about how his alcohol use had increased because of his involvement with cocaine.

I lumped the drummer's alcohol and marijuana consumption together. I didn't say, "Let's have one model for alcohol and another model for pot," because this is a difficult model to construct. You won't find many people's lives getting out of control on marijuana alone unless they smoke ten joints a day, become totally unmotivated, don't pay the bills, and let their lives fall apart.

Knowing this, I merge the two, the alcohol and the marijuana. I work with the progressive nature of that, setting up guidelines for what "out of control" means. I set up a monitoring system. What I did was ask him,

"What does 'out of control' alcohol and marijuana use mean to you?" He gave me these answers: "When I can't practice my drums. When I start to feel physically bad. When I get away from my physical exercise program. When I start to feel bad about myself."

In an outpatient context I can use an approach like the one I used with the drummer. In an inpatient program, where abstinence from all drugs is the policy, I can't. The one thing I never tell clients, however, is that it's okay to use alcohol or marijuana. I say the odds are against them if they try. They will fail to control their use. I give cocaine dependents who want to use alcohol or pot some unpleasant statistics. "During the last five or six years that I have concentrated on cocaine, I've known only a couple of people who have been able to go out and resume smoking marijuana and drinking, without going back to cocaine, or ending up with their lives out of control. Only an exceptional few can do it. The odds are stacked against you. You wouldn't bet on a horse at the racetrack with odds like that. So why bet your life now?"

If a cocaine dependent is involved with other recovering addicts in a therapy group, he won't get far with the argument that alcohol and pot are okay. As soon as he starts talking about his ability to smoke marijuana and drink, he will hear from people who just came back to the group from a relapse caused by the same thinking. Then you are going to have the "us and us" taking place–the good modeling from the other patients who have tried it and failed.

Group reactions are powerful in shaping perceptions and changing thought patterns. However, if a client goes out and tries drinking and smoking, and fails, I always avoid saying "I told you so." I make sure that clients always have a direct line back to me. If things start to go wrong for them they know they can and should call me back to work with them.

This case, while representing the approach I advocate, violates some widely held beliefs about addiction therapy . . . principally that abstinence from all drugs is a prerequisite for treatment. Actually, I believe that total abstinence from all drugs is the way to recovery that works. Yet, if I am too rigid in insisting on that, I may push someone out of treatment. It can alienate him from treatment so severely that psychosocial factors deteriorate to a much worse state before he finally gets into a recovery program. Then treatment will be even more difficult. I think that by being flexible here, I utilized the drummer's pain while creating a system that he could intellectually understand and work.

When I use a treatment approach which does not require abstinence from all drugs I must be very careful about how I present it to the client. What I don't want to happen is for the client to go back out and say to someone, "My therapist said we're just going to watch my alcohol and marijuana use. You should really change therapists because mine is really hip."

Next, we need to examine the internal and external triggers that are involved in rekindling the desire to use cocaine. When I dialogue with a patient, exploring the alcohol and drug issue, I start asking the when, where, and what-is-going-on questions. I find it helpful to list as many details as I can about when this person uses cocaine. "Tell me when you first used. Tell me about the night that you typically used. What night do you start on? What is going on then? Are there times when you find yourself more hungry for cocaine than others?" I ask seemingly innocuous questions, the ones that are often the most revealing. "What are you doing for fun? How are things going in your life? What are you doing over the weekends? How did that go for you when you were using cocaine?" What I begin to see is the set of internal and external triggers that rekindle cocaine hunger and a return to the drug, often they are boredom, stress, and the need for a reward.

One of the things I talk about with clients is euphoric recall. With euphoric recall, we remember all the nice things and we put all the nasty things in the misty background. It is a recurring human phenomenon. Have you ever had someone who severely hurt or damaged you? Does this sound familiar? A friend of yours comes over and says, "Gees, I saw so-and-so the other day." You say, "Yes, I remember him," and then say something nice about him. Then you remember that you hated him. This is similar to how euphoric recall works.

Cocaine addicts always remember the euphoria because it's well-learned. Euphoria starts with the anticipation of copping the drug and "really getting off." This person is high even before the drug enters the body. Any situation that was strongly attached to the use of cocaine will trigger this euphoric recall. Large amounts of money will trigger it. "I get paid. It's Friday night and I always get loaded on Friday nights. Now I go to the bank; I have three hundred dollars in my pocket and I'm going home. I'm going through an area near the person I used to buy from. I'm listening to hard rock music on the radio. (The music is an external anchor.) I start to feel strange. The thought comes to my mind that it sure would be nice to have some cocaine now."

This next story involves alcohol but it reveals how powerful the little triggers to euphoric recall are. It is a fictionalization of things I have heard from many different clients, but it is a good concrete way of illustrating this important phenomenon. It portrays how we can alter our state of consciousness even with a minuscule amount of a chemical.

> *"It is a beautiful day in Oak Forest, Illinois, where I live. I am driving home in my paid-for car, to my beautiful paid-for house in the suburbs. I pull in the driveway; my two kids run out and give me a big hug and say, 'Dad, we're so glad you're home.' I'm home for the weekend. It's a beautiful spring day. I walk into the house and smell a delicious meal being cooked. I kiss my lovely wife, go to the refrigerator, pull out one can of beer, pop the top, take a swallow, and say, 'Boy, do I feel better now.'"*

It wasn't all the marvelous things around me that made me feel better. One swallow of beer did nothing for me physiologically. But it had psychological impact. It altered my state of consciousness in the direction of euphoria. The weekend's started!

It is absolutely essential to insure that the recovering cocaine dependent expects this to happen and knows how to deal with it. I tell him there will be times when he will even dream about cocaine. If this happens, he must look at what is going on in his life. Usually, he'll find that he is going through a high-stress time. I look at what he is *not* doing to maintain sobriety.

I try to anticipate where and when the client will have difficulty with euphoric recall by identifying the events and feeling states that trigger this experience, the high risk situations that he may put himself in. I try to help the recovering addict anticipate the impact of this euphoric recall, and become ready to handle it without succumbing to using cocaine. Then I initiate mental imagery techniques.

A valuable mental imagery technique is "disassociating," moving someone a little bit away from the experience. Have you ridden a roller coaster? Put yourself mentally back into that situation. You're on the roller coaster going toward the top of the first big hill. You're getting ready to go over the top. Now you're going over the top and you can feel the wind in your hair and you get that rush.

Now change your experience. Put yourself on a bench watching yourself go up to the top of the hill and going down the other side. What is the difference? In the first image you relive the experience. In the second image, you watch yourself do it. If you want a nice associative experience as good as, or better than, a cup of coffee in the morning, associate with the roller coaster ride. Now make it clearer, faster, and amplify it. You can start to get that adrenalin rush.

Suppose a person has trouble with a particular situation. He might say, "Every time I go to a wedding reception, I end up snorting cocaine with my friends and we get crazy all night long." My task is to have that person see himself, in his mind, going into the exact situation in a sober state. I have clients practice, both mentally and aloud, the positive alternatives. Similarly, when someone is experiencing drug craving have him disassociate and watch himself. I ask, "What do you see? What is going on?" I have him describe it because that starts to detach him from the brain processes that are so "tuned into" the experience itself. I find that having clients practice disassociating makes it easier for them to handle cravings. Disassociating facilitates detached, objective viewing of an emotional situation.

Exposing clients to drug paraphernalia and practicing mental imagery involving drugs can sometimes trigger dangerous feelings and craving. I want to make sure the client can deal with those feelings before he leaves the session. So, whenever I do mental imagery with a cocaine addict or a chemically addicted person on an outpatient basis, I always do it at the beginning of the session. I never do it on a Friday because the weekend is the greatest danger period for cravings and relapse to drug use.

Another technique I use, especially early in the program, involves a twenty-five cent notebook. I ask my clients to do something very simple. I say, "Look, anytime you have a dream or you wake up in the middle of the night, and you've got clammy hands and you're perspiring and you can smell ether vapor in your nostril, or anytime you're out in the world and you notice that you're starting to get that craving, write down whatever you think and feel at that time in the notebook." This helps the client detach from the feeling, step back from the compulsion.

I do a lot of journaling. It's a proven technique that works. Journaling is a challenge because for many cocaine dependents the idea of doing something everyday, or even the concept of living "one day at a time," must be learned in the recovery program. Sometimes "everyday" and "today" are just too low-gear for the cocaine addict. I remember a cocaine patient keeping track of his daily progress who said, "You know, CC, I've been straight for three days." He looked as though three days was awful. "Three is too small a number," he said. "You know, I just don't . . . three days is nothing!" And I said, "Well, what do you like?" He said, "Well, you know, I really like big numbers, like half a million. Now that's my kind of number."

So we talked and thought about that and I got him a little calculator. Every time I saw him around the unit from then on I asked him to tell me how many seconds he had been straight. Well, those seconds added up quickly.

In a very short time he was accumulating fractions of a million and millions of seconds. He had a number that was relevant to him that he didn't want to violate. This is also an illustration of an idea I mentioned earlier, taking what a client gives you and finding a way to work with it, to use it.

If I have people who have a craving that is so bad that their emotions have completely overridden their intellect, I use an equation. It is: *thoughts* + *emotions* = *behavior.* When a cocaine addict is having a lot of difficulty, the one thing he can control is his behavior. We all know how this works. Whenever we think and feel something, it influences how we behave at that moment. Every cocaine client must become aware that if we turn this equation around, if we engage in productive behavior, we alter our thoughts and emotions positively.

I have patients go through some reverse rituals. If someone has a freebase pipe, I have him go through the ritual of breaking it. Trash the paraphernalia. I have had people tell me that after their first time through treatment, they found themselves scraping the pipe in hopes of finding enough in there to smoke. I try to get these souvenirs of cocaine addiction out of the way. There is a reason people hang onto them. If they have accepted that they can't use again, it's easy for them to get rid of the pipe. If they "hem and haw" about it, say that they want to keep it to remember the bad times, I worry. There is still a part of them that would like to use cocaine again.

Cocaine has a recognizable smell. It is labeled as a white, crystalline, odorless powder. But when you extract cocaine you often use a solvent (acetone or ether), and it will have a strong and unique odor. People who freebase and inject will describe the ether smell as recognizable and attractive for them. Professionals first discovered how profound the smell is just a few years ago.

I worked with an anesthesiologist who would only get hungry for cocaine when he had to go into the operating room. He started to smell the anesthetic and it would "drive him nuts." He didn't understand it until he made the connection that one of his anchors was smell. Ron Siegele, in California, has worked with a synthetic cocaine aroma which can be made by mixing three inert chemicals. During early recovery, therapists have tried allowing the recovering addict to smell that vial *ad lib*. The theory is that it may have a desensitizing property. And it does seem to take away some of the cocaine hunger for some individuals.

A technique that I have used with good results is to pull out a little white powder in a group. Just with this simple action I immediately create an emotional clone of what it feels like as a recovering addict to be around cocaine. The response is instantaneous. It's a feeling of anxiety, of expectation. You're getting off already; the adrenalin is starting to flow, like you're just getting ready to snort a line. As soon as the client feels that, I ask him to whip out that twenty-five cent notebook I mentioned earlier and to write about it. I say, "I want you to tell me where you are, who you're with, what's going on, and anything else about what's going on."

Although this is in and of itself an intervention, it also is a learning experience. What I first caused the client to do was drop the intellectual mode and react emotionally, more similar to how events are going to be responded to in the real world. But then, I suddenly ask him to click into an intellectual mode of functioning. Having to intellectually describe the experience pulls the client back out of the kinesthetic-emotional mode, defocusing from the emotion back into the intellect. The whole approach is based on the recognition that when the intellect is in control, the client has a better chance of handling a situation that's pulling him in the direction of drug use.

Cocaine often has become a key element in the dependent's self-reward system. Once this is understood, clients can usually learn to reshape their own behavior and improve their chances of staying off drugs. I worked with a lawyer who was captivated by cocaine as a self-reward. He said things like, "When I win a big case I buy cocaine and go to the bar with other lawyers. We do a lot of cocaine and this is my reward. The time I buy is when I win a case." Winning a big case would almost instantly create an intense cocaine hunger. To recover, he had to be sensitive to that. We worked on developing alternative responses to winning. Number one was to stay out of the bar to begin with. If a big case was coming up, he learned to schedule a meeting for afterward and a positive activity for that evening, not a self-defeating one.

Another thing I do if a recovering cocaine dependent must go into a risky environment, is make sure he takes someone from the program. I tell them to drive themselves–so that they don't go with two other crazies who are going to be snorting cocaine until 4 A.M., leaving them waiting for a ride home. This approach is called "action planning" or problem solving. It teaches the cocaine dependent how to create a way out of dangerous situations. Action planning gives the power to interrupt a developing pattern.

I make a special point to look at any seemingly benign stimulants the cocaine addict may be using. Although having accepted cocaine's problems, clients sometimes take diet pills on the side, or have a high intake of caffeine and nicotine. Nicotine is a powerful stimulant. If nicotine were snorted in the same quantities as cocaine it would kill. It is more toxic. Nicotine is a potent central nervous system stimulant with addictive properties. If a large amount of caffeinated coffee and nicotine is taken in, cocaine dependents start to get that old stimulation–buzz and excitement.

When Cocaine is Part of a Relationship

In treating a cocaine addict I always work with the "significant other" whenever possible, the spouse or lover. Is cocaine a common denominator in their relationship? This is the first and most important question to ask. If cocaine is what the couple is giving one another, the typical progression of events is not drastically different from that of the couple that argues, has a bottle of champagne, goes to bed together, and has a honeymoon for a week. The anxiety builds. They blow up at one another, go out, get drunk and then make love.

Suppose I have a patient who has been in inpatient care and is returning home on a pass. It's the final weekend before discharge and the day is going to be spent with the wife, girlfriend, or whomever. They jump into bed and in five minutes it is all over. But they have the euphoric recall of what cocaine did for sex early in the addictive process. They may recall that they used to stay up all night long and "get it on." Now it's over in five minutes. Both of them, or at least one of them, is thinking, "Damn, it would be great to have a gram right now."

Treating one partner is especially difficult if both partners are cocaine dependent. If this is the case, many new issues arise. They may have emotionally distanced one another. How can I enhance their intimacy, to allow them to deal with the sexual problem? Usually there is nothing wrong physiologically. It just has become part of their psychology that every time they have sex they think about cocaine. It's another anchor.

I explore ways to enhance the intimate relationship by asking, "How can you create a nice romantic evening? What things can be done to prolong the evening, to make it rewarding?" Carefully planning a romantic evening together helps. This should only be used if there is true caring in the relationship, and only as an adjunct to couples counseling.

I do a little teaching. I explain the fact that people who do a lot of drugs together lose many of the most important aspects of sexuality. Sexuality has many layers and tiers. There are caring, inclusion, acceptance, friendship, and genital response. In chemical dependency you lose it from top to bottom. The last thing you lose is the genital response. I start working on the caring, inclusion, acceptance, and friendship. I get them to invest in planning romance, candlelight dinners, nice evenings together. I encourage them to do more foreplay because it prolongs the sexual act. It is intimate and enjoyable. It also creates excitement in the relationship–something cocaine did. I find that these simple techniques work better than anything else.

One of the issues I often have to deal with is a client's guilt and shame about some of the sexual activities they were engaged in while using drugs: wife and husband swapping, and group sex. All this is part of the craziness of the cocaine high and cocaine toxicity. There will often be cheating and extramarital affairs. Many recovering cocaine addicts put their marriages "right on the verge" by getting involved in affairs just so they can get the excitement they crave. This is another reason why I try to treat the whole family–get them all involved in recovery.

Unfortunately, there may be no formal organization in your area that accepts and works with the family problems of the cocaine addict. For example, Al-Anon is an effective family program, but in your area or situation they may not want to deal with the family of a cocaine user. If you have Families Anonymous in your area, it is a reasonably effective alternative.

In summary, recovery is something the client learns to do by and for himself alone. The treatment of cocaine addiction begins with a process of professional regulation of the client but this is only temporary. Patients come to me and ask if they are addicted to cocaine and what to do about it. And I teach them how to get straight. However, the goal of my cocaine treatment is to get the client to where he can effectively manage his own life, soberly and effectively. I want my clients to become self-motivated and start solving problems for themselves. Somewhere along the route to full client responsibility our relationship changes. Instead of telling how to do it, I become more a consultant. What I am describing is an educational process.

The quality of this educational approach is what distinguishes successful recovery programs from ineffectual ones. The question which must always be asked about a program's content is whether or not the ideas and coping strategies learned will truly help the client create a new and fulfilling life without drugs. The strategies I have explained in this chapter all address the fundamental problem of the recovering cocaine addict: how to say good-bye to the love affair.

Chapter 8

NUTRITION AND EXERCISE

In treating the cocaine addict, it must be understood that nutrition and physical exercise are cornerstones of recovery. When we start to look at the experience of cocaine addiction, we can view it from many perspectives. In some ways, cocaine addiction looks like an eating disorder. Cocaine also disrupts feelings of well-being by impacting negatively on endorphin levels. Most important, when a person's physical well-being and nutritional well-being are strong, it is much easier for him to believe there is a benevolent, higher power. In other words, physical exercise and nutrition are important pieces of the acceptance process as well as important pieces of reestablishing a positive self-image and a more viable, functioning neurotransmitter system.

Cocaine is an anorexigenic drug. While a person is using cocaine, the appetite is drastically reduced. It is not uncommon for a cocaine addict to enter treatment in an emaciated state. This emaciated state involves reductions in vitamins and other important body nutrients. It is not uncommon for a cocaine addict to have lost more than 20% of the body's normal weight, considering body frame and height.

When a cocaine addict enters treatment after having used cocaine for extended periods of time, he may be not only malnourished and underweight, but he may also have a distorted body image. This body image is sometimes similar to that of an anorexic. The cocaine addict may talk very much like the anorexic and display the anorexic's distorted body image. This body image may be described as feelings of body weight being ideal or maybe not even being thin enough, although the client may have lost a tremendous amount of weight and be well-below normal body mass. Cocaine addicts may say that their buttocks and thighs are not quite perfect. Again, these are statements often heard from anorexics.

When the cocaine addict enters treatment and has been off cocaine for two days, we see behavior that looks more akin to bulimia or gross overeating. The cocaine addict may on days two, three, four and even on the fifth day of treatment, crave highly refined carbohydrates. In other words, the addict may want to eat tremendous quantities of products containing sugar, foods like ice cream, cakes and cookies. This creates several problems for the cocaine addict. First of all, I do not want the cocaine addict to consume vast amounts of carbohydrates and gain large amounts of weight extremely early in recovery. Second, I am very concerned about the cocaine addict's mood swings during this crucial stage. A well-balanced, low-sugar, diet is especially important to emotional stability.

In regard to physical exercise, the cocaine addict will often have difficulty with compliance. It is, therefore, necessary to get the cocaine addict involved in a physical exercise regimen that is social and exciting, but yet has some elements of aerobic conditioning. What I really want to produce for the cocaine addict is a way to have fun in recovery while stimulating the endorphin and enkephalin system, and a way of doing all this in the company of others who are also interested in recovery.

Nutrition

Many cocaine addicts are adult children of alcoholics. It has been estimated that at least 50% to 60% of cocaine addicts come from a home where there is some additional dysfunction, secondary to the alcoholism and/or drug addiction. For example, Janet Woititz noted there is an increased incidence of attention deficit disorders within the homes of alcoholics. In the adult cocaine addict, attention deficits may go unnoticed, especially when average or above-average intelligence levels enable compensating for this disorder.

One red flag that signals the presence of an attention deficit is the cocaine addict's subjective experience of feeling calmer and more focused while using cocaine. In other words, cocaine is acting in the same fashion that Ritalin may act within the brain pharmacologically. It is a paradoxical effect, a reversal of the typical stimulant effect of cocaine.

Attention disorders may exist among cocaine addicts alongside cognitive disabilities and mood sweeps, especially in early recovery. However, I really do not want to emphasize the cocaine addict's inability to understand a program of recovery. In nearly all cases, good nutrition helps minimize a patient's cognitive difficulties and mood swings.

During the detoxification stage it is often helpful to use fruits *ad lib* because they provide carbohydrates that are not refined, nutrients which are more slowly absorbed and better-tolerated by the body. This type of carbohydrate does not exaggerate mood swings, which may be a problem with sugar products. It has also proven helpful to provide fluids to help flush out, or detoxify, the system while the cocaine addict is in detox.

With experience, I have become concerned about other stimulant drugs, such as caffeine and nicotine. Various programs have policies on caffeinated coffee and the use or non-use of nicotine. Regardless of these policies, it must be understood that when the patient returns to the real world after treatment, he or she may smoke more cigarettes and consume coffee and other caffeinated beverages at a much greater rate than during treatment. In the past, some of my clients have gone to NA, AA and CA meetings and consumed ten cups of caffeinated coffee with a half-a-pack of cigarettes and then wondered why they started to have a craving for cocaine. The combination of stimulants, such as nicotine and caffeine, around cues such as conversations about procuring and using the drug cocaine, led to a powerful craving which could easily be a trigger for relapse.

In recent years, there has been a growing body of data on the use of nutritional supplements for cocaine addicts. Such supplements as the Matrix Technology product with the registered trademarks *Tropamine* and *Saave* have brought a new technology to adjunctive treatment. These nutritional supplements are nonaddicting, nonmood-altering, nonprescription amino acids that are loaded into the body to help reduce the deficits in norepinephrine, dopamine, serotonin and to also make the endorphin and enkephalins more readily bioavailable during early recovery. In the new literature on adjunctive procedures to primary treatment the work of Joel Robertson at the Robertson Clinic in Bay City, Michigan is significant. Dr. Robertson has come up with a system that allows the most specific approach to assessing the nutritional and physical exercise needs of the cocaine addict.

Physical Exercise

Early recovery is often a time of existential crisis. When a person is wondering about issues of life and death and is feeling empty inside, the usual symptoms are those of loneliness, isolation and boredom. Cocaine addicts often express concern over feelings of extreme boredom in treatment and early recovery. This can be understood in light of the fact that their lifestyles were very addictive. They were often engaged in illegal practices with a drug that is three- to five-times as valuable as gold. The drug itself is very much a stimulant type of drug. My own concern with boredom is this: I do not want cocaine addicts to go out and undermine their recovery by getting involved in activities such as sexual acting out and gambling. It is important to help them find stimulating physical activities that can provide attractive alternatives to the cocaine lifestyle. It can be helpful to schedule these exercises during the times when cravings are anticipated, such as weekends and Friday evening.

This need for exciting alternatives is illustrated by a cocaine addict I'll call George, whom I treated a few years ago. Every week George would come into my office and tell me that he just knew that I wouldn't let him do what he had in mind. I often placed certain expectations, rules and limitations on his activities.

One week he walked in, looked at me and said, "C.C., I know you will never let me do this." And I said, "What is it this week, George?" George replied, "I want to skydive." I said, "I think that is a wonderful idea, but there are only two rules: you must take lessons and you must wear a parachute." For several months, George and some other recovering cocaine addicts went to an AA breakfast every Sunday and then proceeded to a small field outside of Chicago where they would work out for a while and then skydive.

The moral to this is that Sunday was formerly a time when George felt lonely and bored. Now he had an exciting activity that involved self-help and recovering people. It was both exciting to him and involved physical exercise.

Physical exercise that is fun as well as challenging is a very important cornerstone of recovery. It was Norman Cousins who talked about the therapeutic use of laughter in inducing increased endorphins and enhancing immune system functioning. Similarly, there have been many research studies on how physical exercise enhances endorphin and enkephalin levels. It appears that physical exercise is a sometimes-ignored, yet critical, part of recovery from cocaine addiction. When a person starts to appreciate feeling well and can associate these positive feelings with the behaviors that are currently part of his life–self-help, treatment and other recovery and family-oriented activities–there is a positive and productive result of physical exercise that directly enhances all areas of recovery.

There are some important considerations in physical exercise programs of early recovery. For example, it has been shown that some cocaine addicts may have cardiovascular problems. We do know that many cocaine addicts, while using cocaine, will experience angina-type chest pains. This is due to constriction of the major coronary arteries. It has also been discovered that chronic cocaine use can cause a narrowing of these coronary arteries causing, at times, 20- to 25-year-old cocaine addicts to be candidates for double coronary by-pass operations. It is critical, in early recovery, to have the cardiovascular status of the cocaine addict examined by a physician. In a treatment setting, this type of evaluation is often done during the detoxification phase. Medical clearance is then written allowing the cocaine addict to participate in more vigorous exercise during rehabilitation and the ensuing recovery phases.

Even during the first few days of recovery, however, the element of physical exercise must not be overlooked. Low impact exercise is often appropriate during the detoxification phase. Many cocaine addicts, after a binge, when their body has been in a "fight-or-flight" mode, will exhibit symptoms that almost look like heroin withdrawal. You will see tightened neck, back, and leg muscles. These muscles will not only be tight, but often very tender. This will cause newly recovering cocaine addicts to exhibit pill-seeking behavior. They may ask the nursing staff or physician for aspirin, Tylenol or such medications as Valium.

This complaint about sore muscles may be confusing to the clinical staff since it looks so much like withdrawal from opiate drugs–heroin, dilaudid, morphine and fentanyl. Instead of administering the aspirin or Valium, it may be prudent to engage the cocaine addict in yoga-type or prerunning, stretching exercises. This encourages the addict to relate to staff members as well as to defocus from the tenderness in his neck, back and legs. It also teaches skills which can help relieve minor pain and discomfort, without using drugs.

All in all, the recovery process involves a serious commitment to well-being. This well-being involves not only professional treatment and self-help, but physical exercise and nutrition. Physical exercise and nutrition, when looked at as a self-maintenance strategy, is a form of self-love. In recovery, as we start to care for and to value ourselves, careful nutrition and physical exercise will make more and more sense. They will help create values and beliefs which are much easier to live with. Loving ourselves, we will find love for our fellow recovering addicts and the significant others in our lives.

Chapter 9

PREVENTING RELAPSE

For recovering cocaine addicts who have completed a treatment program and are in outpatient aftercare programs, months two through six represent a major window of relapse to drug use. This is a tough period for cocaine addicts as well as those addicted to other chemicals, 60 days through 180 days into recovery. For cocaine addicts, this high risk relapse period seems to peak about 30 days sooner than it does for alcoholics. The 15 day period from 60 to 85 days into recovery seems to be particularly hazardous for cocaine addicts.

To understand cocaine relapse we must look beyond the addictive substance itself. There is a psychological dimension to the relapse dynamic. A recovering cocaine dependent can reach a point where his world seems to be falling apart, when he is tormented by a feeling that he is going to die, go crazy, or return to drugs. And returning to cocaine is no longer an option. Recovering cocaine addicts in this psychological state have accidents, physical problems, emotional problems, or even attempt suicide.

There are clues to an impending relapse. An important one is any dramatic change in a client's reactions, especially a client who has been through detox, is in rehab and is working a good recovery program. Suddenly, this person may seem highly agitated. Besides this recurrence of "overamping," a characteristic of cocaine dependence, I sometimes see a return of olfactory pseudohallucinations (smelling cocaine), sleep problems such as insomnia or waking up during the night and not being able to go back to sleep, and disturbed eating patterns–undereating or overeating. The recovery honeymoon is over.

Some therapists interpret this sudden disruption of the forward progression of recovery as a purposeful device to avoid facing some distressing program requirement, for example, a self-help or therapy group which has touched a nerve. This "regression," or backward movement, is sometimes dealt with by directly confronting the client, although it is not a method I recommend. My approach to closing this window of relapse has been to teach clients to anticipate these reactions and to minimize their impact, if they do occur, with proper nutrition, physical exercise to deal with the anxiety and a tight program structure that keeps clients moving and carefully monitored.

The following case history illustrates how relapse sometimes arises during this critical period.

Two months had passed since Linda graduated from a residential treatment program, after having been diagnosed as addicted to both cocaine and alcohol. Her treatment plan included two NA and two AA meetings per week. She also had established solid nutritional and physical exercise programs.

Still, part of Linda yearned for the "high life." One weekend Marsha, an old friend and a college sorority sister, came to town and phoned her. The call triggered Linda's memory of the sorority, college, and the old party scene. Eagerly, she agreed to meet Marsha at a familiar hangout, "Gary's Duck Inn and Waddle Out." There, Marsha convinced Linda that a few cocktails could never hurt. Besides, her problem really was cocaine, not alcohol. Cocaine was the only thing she had ever really lost control of.

Weeks passed and Linda felt more and more guilty about her relapse. She attended fewer meetings and didn't return her sponsor's phone calls. One Friday night, feeling confused and anxious, she again went back to the bar seeking some relief. There she ran into Tom. Tom and Linda had been involved in a cocaine romance prior to her treatment. Although part of her knew better, Tom's offer of coke and sympathy was too much to turn down.

Tom and Linda went back to her place and snorted line after line of cocaine. Seduced by the drug and Tom, and unbalanced from not working her recovery program, Linda was wired again. She had taken up where she had left off–in the spiral of cocaine addiction.

The Relapse Dynamic

In the case of Linda, there were external social pressures to use cocaine. These pressures are just one of several events which might trigger a relapse. The common idea or theme linking together most relapse precipitators is "cues." Cues are the people, places, things, and ideas that remind us, often through feelings, of some behavior we learned in the past. To a considerable degree relapse is controlled by the internal cues and external cues I mentioned briefly in Chapter 1.

In recovery, loneliness, fatigue, and hunger all function as internal cues that can trigger cocaine relapse. In our work with alcoholism we learned the importance of "H.A.L.T." Feeling Hungry, Angry, Lonely, or Tired can cause an urge to drink. These are internal cues which are equally relevant to cocaine addiction, even more so perhaps in the case of hunger, a feeling that the cocaine addict may have forgotten. Cocaine suppresses hunger. Moreover, the recovering person may not have learned to deal with strong emotions such as anger, nor how to cope with loneliness.

A very common thought pattern in response to loneliness, an internal cue, is:

> *"Every time I used to feel blue, I snorted two lines of cocaine and felt better. I remember my friends saying to me, 'If you do cocaine, what a sexy drug; you can have a lot of chicks or guys.' It's Saturday night now and I'm all by myself. What I used to do on Saturday night was freebase and drink a fifth of Jack Daniels and smoke some reefer. Now I'm just sitting here feeling bored and lonely. What am I thinking about? The drugs."*

External cues are outside us, embedded in the physical environment of people, places and things. The good news is that since external cues are visible and concrete, we often have more control over them than we do over internal cues. Our principal means of controlling the effect of external cues is avoidance. In essence, there are people, places, and things we must avoid in order to stay sober and clean. For example, certain people must be avoided because our friendship with them was based upon using drugs. When we are around these people we are naturally going to think about drugs.

Let's consider some other external cues for relapse. A large sum of money is an external trigger. I find that if a cocaine addict gets paid on Friday and he made seven hundred dollars, he will often put two or three hundred dollars in his pocket. So when a client receives a large sum of money, on payday for example, I have him go straight to the bank or, better yet, have the check sent to a bank.

I eliminate bank cards, too, if I can. I go through a ritual of having them broken up and thrown away. I put clients on a budget. By putting them on a budget, they don't have that anchor in the pocket. I try to have them carry no more than thirty or forty dollars in cash. Most people don't need to walk around with more cash than that.

Familiar songs are external cues; all the old heroin songs like, " . . . when you're married to H, you're married for life . . . ." And the British Blues bands–it's like you can just "get down" with them. They alter your state of consciousness. Have you ever heard Eric Clapton's cocaine song? You can "get off" on that song without cocaine. It's an upbeat piece of music and you "get into" that. I try to work with people, especially at high risk times, to tune into easy listening. Listen to a sports station, a talk show. Do something different. Break the pattern.

External cues, especially things associated with drug use, are so powerful that sometimes an addict begins to enter a euphoric state before the drug enters the body, certainly before it hits the brain in sufficient concentration to produce a physical effect. Think about the alcoholic I mentioned earlier who goes home and pulls out that first beer, and after taking just one swallow responds, "Ah, boy do I feel better now." The one swallow does nothing physiologically, but the external cues produce the effect.

Lenny Bruce clearly described a powerful external cue in his autobiography, *How To Talk Dirty and Influence People* (1965). Before he went on stage, Lenny Bruce would mix 4 mg. Dilaudid with a milliliter of amphetamine and put it in a syringe. According to Lenny, he knew he was OK when he put the needle in his arm and saw "the rose." The rose, the blood pedalling back and registering in the syringe, was an external cue. Before he even injected the drug into his system he was already off.

I look to the past to understand a client's external cues, to the future to understand his internal ones. External cues reemerge as repeat performances of past history. By carefully studying a client's background and lifestyle, I can usually find a way to nullify the worst external cues. In contrast, internal cues emerge spontaneously, often taking new forms in response to new and novel situations. With internal cues there is always that element of surprise. To deal with them effectively I must be more like a weather forecaster than an historian, always looking ahead to tomorrow. In either case, though, the client is instrumental in pinpointing the exact cues which represent the greatest danger for relapse. His full cooperation is absolutely vital.

Changing the Pattern

In treating cocaine addicts I repeatedly hear, "When I feel depressed I use. When I am lonely I use. It's Friday night and I don't intend to use cocaine, but I'm sitting alone with nothing to do. I feel empty–bored and empty." What thought comes to mind next? "If I use cocaine I won't feel bored and empty."

For example, Martin, a cocaine addict, thought he would never use cocaine again–not after all he had learned from his therapist.

But, one Saturday night Martin decided that he felt just too tired and lonely to go to his NA meeting. He decided to stay home, to rest and wallow in his isolation. He heard his sponsor's voice saying, "The time to go to a meeting is the time you least feel like going. That's when you need it the most." Martin didn't heed his sponsor's advice.

Around 9:00 P.M. Martin started to play some old music on the stereo, the music he used to play on Saturday night when he stayed at home alone doing cocaine. He noticed that he was feeling anxious and found himself picking up the telephone twice. He was thinking about calling Lance, his former dealer. Each time he resisted the temptation.

As time went by the "blues" kept rolling in. Martin felt as if he had to call Lance, go crazy, or die. All three were nonrecovery options. Eventually, out of desperation, he called Lance, who was all-too-happy to sell Martin cocaine. You see, Martin and Lance had been lovers and had always done cocaine together. When Martin admitted his problem, Lance had introspected, wondering what this meant in terms of his own cocaine use. Now Lance convinced Martin that neither had a problem. There were many others who had worse habits than they ever had.

Although relapse itself is not an intellectual experience, I teach clients intellectual strategies for dealing with the risk, for instance, avoiding the reduction in positive options that results from being in a room full of people snorting cocaine. A few simple changes may be all that's required to avoid or neutralize high risk situations. Identifying what these changes are and how to make them is a part of what I call self-discovery. It involves always striving for objectivity about one's own past and what it means. To further this quest, I ask my clients to take a sheet of paper and list the places they should avoid, the people they should avoid, and the things in their lives that need changing. And then, on the other side of the paper, they put down how they're going to do it. It sounds simple. But this simple activity has profound implications for recovery. I suggest doing this either individually with a counselor or in a recovery group. When this is done by group members, the list provides concrete and challenging material for discussion.

So, when we really think about relapse, we see that it is not so much actually doing the drug, but getting into an environmental context and state of mind, where we have the old expectations and perceptions, where the setting and the set are just right for using drugs. If we let this happen, it reduces our options. This explains why relapse is not an intellectual experience, a subject for conceptual analysis. You may premeditate it, but for the most part when you're in a position where the old cues are going off, it's a kinesthetic or emotional experience. It's the "great attracter" within a chaotic pattern.

Structuring time is one way of "changing the pattern." Like Martin, there are recovering cocaine addicts who spend time in their former neighborhoods, meet the same people, and listen to the same music. An effective recovery program requires changing these behaviors. For example, some of us have the "high school Fridays." In high school, Friday night was always my party night. So when I entered college life, Friday was always the hardest night to deal with. If that is the reality of the cocaine dependent, the Friday night pattern must be broken.

As a therapist, I am always attentive to patterns of cocaine use and try to devise ways to disrupt and replace these patterns. I identify high risk situations through my dialogues with the client. If I listen carefully to what the client says, he will reveal when his high risk times are. I find out when they "cop," and when they'll be in situations where they'll think about "copping." Usually these will be Friday nights, a lot of Thursday nights, and if they are "really hip" they'll know that their dealer usually "cops" on Wednesday or Thursday night and they can buy that night before the cocaine gets all "cut" up.

Cravings

Craving is implicated in nearly all relapses. The development of a hunger or craving is characteristic of any drug that is abused. People start to crave it. The craving associated with cocaine dependence is profound. I've often had people call me up and say, "It's the only thing I can think of. I can see a picture in my mind of myself doing cocaine. I can see myself buying it and laying the lines out, filling up the pipe . . . ." They're having an associative experience in which they're actually living it again. When people have an associative experience, they become more emotional and less intellectual. They are overwhelmed by the profound sense of "I would really like to go out and get some of this drug."

To the cocaine dependent, the drug experience is an anchored one, another concept central to relapse prevention. An example of an anchored experience is chewing aluminum foil on a cavity. What happens when you think about that? Or, how about someone taking her fingernails and raking them down a chalk board? I don't have to give you the aluminum foil or the chalk board. You have that experience "stashed" in your brain. It's important to remember that the drug experience is similarly "stashed" in the brain of every chemically dependent person.

This anchored experience concept helps explain why eighty-three percent of the recovering cocaine dependents say they just can't resist cocaine if they are near it. "I don't want to use, but if I put myself in physical proximity to cocaine, I can't say no to it." Physical proximity to cocaine is perhaps the most powerful anchor. Cocaine dependents even seem to have a sixth sense for cocaine. Many can walk into a room and sense everyone in the room who is using.

When the recovering addict is in the presence of cocaine and manages to avoid using it, there is still the danger of a destructive internal cue being triggered: resentment. This becomes "adjustment disorder with resentment." This trance-like state is induced when you put a cocaine addict around the old external cues that trigger his craving.

Driving past the dealer's house is an anchor. I learned about this type of anchor from an insurance salesman in Chicago. He told me, "I had to alter my downtown Loop route because every time I went past my old watering hole, I'd start feeling really weird. I'd feel real strange, right in the pit of my stomach." What he found was his own intervention: he stopped going that way. He took a different route–went around the corner–and it alleviated his anxiety. By encouraging the recovering addict to stay out of places where he shouldn't be, I start to break the pattern. He must, by all means, avoid being around cocaine.

Some people like to test themselves by setting up high risk situations. I hear such stories all the time: "I was just riding in the neighborhood–just happened to be in that area–and I was thinking about my friend Johnny, who I always got my cocaine from. Johnny is a very good friend of mine and I miss having the chance to talk to him.

So I go over to Johnny's house and I notice that as I get one block from Johnny's house I am gripping the steering wheel so hard my knuckles are white. My car is going a little faster than it usually does. I come screeching into Johnny's driveway and I go inside. In the process I have already convinced myself that it's okay to use cocaine. I can 'blow it off' tomorrow. I can just do it for tonight and worry about it later." Or he may say, "It's okay to snort as long as I stay away from the pipe." Or, "I'll only do a gram and quit by 11 P.M."

If I can identify the triggers, they will usually imply the use of specific types of interventions. I can structure those high risk times with alternative activities, activities that are helpful to the family, self-help, fun activities. I work on keeping that person's life balanced.

Boredom and Stress

The cocaine addict has several addictions, and all of them are to excitement. So, boredom is always a big risk. The scenario goes like this: "I worked hard this week and suddenly it's Friday night. I have no social plans. It's 9 P.M. and I'm bored. What I would like is a little excitement. Then I play a little mind game with myself that I've played before. I say, 'I'm going to go out and buy a gram. That's all I'm going to use.' Then sometime around Sunday, when I have gone through about a quarter of an ounce, I realize that, once again, my scheme didn't work."

What we are seeing again is an old pattern. What happens when cocaine addicts are under stress? They use chemicals to maintain internal controls. Although many people use depressant drugs like alcohol when they are under stress, cocaine, a stimulant, may have a calming effect on the addict. The treatment challenge is to help them acquire alternative behaviors. Again, break the pattern; it's fundamental.

Managing Cocaine Debt

Another precipitator of relapse falls under the category "returning to work." What do I do when I have a client who works for U-NAME-IT Company and owes two thousand dollars to people who work in the plant? He is getting ready to leave an inpatient environment and return to the work place. He's scared and emotional. He knows the people he owes money to are going to come up to him with a deal. "There is a way you can start to pay me back. I have a good deal for you. I got an ounce in my locker and you can cut a couple grams out for yourself, if you like, and sell the rest."

To help negate this relapse threat, I use role playing to help cocaine dependents develop alternative responses. One alternative response is to make arrangements to pay off the debt. I think that taking the initiative is the best tool here. They usually have the phone numbers of the people they owe money to. While they're still in treatment I have them telephone them and make arrangements to repay the debt. "I will pay you so many dollars every paycheck."

There is one thing to be careful of. You don't want them to try to pay back too much, too soon. Paying cocaine debts back too fast causes problems in other areas of life which can trigger relapse, like being unable to pay the rent or feed the kids. This is another reason why the budgeting process is so important. A good budget will permit the client to meet his basic needs, while keeping cocaine creditors off his back.

Despite a strong fear of returning to work, recovering addicts can be shown how to take charge of the situation. "I have a plan. Every payday I pay back Joe and Mark twenty-five dollars each." It may take a year or two. However, after three or four months a client may start resenting having to pay this money back. At least I have "bought them some time," though, and have taken the heat off. Later, I can start to work with the resentment. The problem evolves, evolves and evolves. Solutions require time.

Telephone Intervention

When someone calls on the phone and says he's experiencing an irresistible urge to use cocaine, I have him try to disassociate. I can do it over the phone. Association is reliving it, or being there. Disassociation is being able to step back and watch yourself and watch what you are doing.

Let me share a story to illustrate this. I want to put a disclaimer on this story. I do not recommend doing this, but in this instance it was all I had to work with.

I had a twenty-seven-year-old rock musician for a client who also owned a cattle ranch. I picked him up from a cardiac care unit. He had freebased thirty-two hundred dollar's worth of cocaine in less than forty-eight hours and they thought he had a heart attack. It turned out that he was having a cardiac arrhythmia with associated chest pain.

He called me up, two days out of the hospital (we had set up an appointment for the next day) and said,

> *"CC, I just can't make it. I think I'm going to kill myself." I said all the injunctions . . . "It's not okay to*

kill yourself . . . ," went through all the dialogue, and determined it was remote ideation. He had no plan and appeared to be asking for help. So then I said, "M--, I want you to do one thing. I'm on the north side of town and I want you to meet me at my home office. It's thirty minutes away from your house, but it will take me one hour to get there. I want you to clean your living room. (I knew this person was a bachelor and what his house looked like.) Then get in your car and come to see me."

I rushed home, in forty-five minutes or an hour. I got there, waited for M--, and nothing happened. When I called him he said, "You know what? I cleaned up my living room and I started to feel so good I decided I didn't need to see you."

This story illustrates how positive behavior can reshape thoughts and emotions. Any time we are dealing with craving, if we can start to disassociate a little bit and get into nearly any positive alternative behavior, the feeling eases.

Is Willpower an Option?

Willpower is no insurance policy against relapse. All that willpower and self-control do is prolong the agony. Trying to cure cocaine addiction with willpower is similar to trying to cure diarrhea with willpower. It simply doesn't work.

I find that patients who have been through treatment two and three times are often working a willpower model. They selectively hear only the things that support that model. When they finally begin showing real progress they may be responding to some of the seeds that were planted during earlier treatments. "Oh! I remember!" takes on a new meaning.

After abandoning the willpower model, patients reach the point where they can say and believe, "I'm a cocaine addict." And they can say it three or four times without it getting caught in their throats. They start saying, "Gee, it's not so bad that I'm a cocaine addict because I've had to learn a whole lot. I've had to adjust my lifestyle so that I feel productive. I have something to look forward to in my life."

When I observe clients, I find how they behave is more important than what they say. Are they comfortable with abstinence? I see people who work a willpower model as though a war was going on inside. The most miserable people I have ever seen are addicts who try to work a willpower model. We call it a "dry drunk" or "white knuckle abstinence." There is "a piece in their head" that says, "Okay, experience has taught me that I can't do cocaine. But there is still a piece of me that says, 'NO, I AM NOT a cocaine addict.'" There is constant conflict, double messages, and discordance inside the individual.

I think both over-compliance and resistance stem from the internal turmoil that occurs when a person is working a willpower model, instead of "turning it over, to let go and let God." If we look at compliance, which in my mind may be another form of resistance, the body and mind are discordant.

Where is the energy going in this model? The energy is all internal, expended trying to figure out what is going on. They think, "Every day I feel bad. I feel like I'm on edge all the time. I'm always thinking about using. I got a piece of me that is fueling the hope that maybe I'll be able to use again. I'm not comfortable with me, not comfortable in any way."

When I start seeing these things, the words I notice are, "I should, I ought, I can, I could." All these are willpower words. They imply control over my addiction. "I should be able to control this thing."

People can't recover until they accept that they have a problem. You're not actually in a recovery program until you've gone through the acceptance stage. You can't relapse from a relapse. Suppose I am starting a treatment plan with someone. I say, "Yes, you should make four meetings a week, and your wife should do this, and I suggest that you go to aftercare for a year." He starts bargaining with me. This is a sign of resistance. If someone has accepted that he is truly cocaine dependent, he will logically want to use every available modality to deal with this addiction. When a person is unwilling to do that, it is symptomatic of the war inside.

Something positive happens when a person accepts that he is chemically dependent, a cocaine addict. There is congruence between the body and the mind. All his energy can be channeled into a beautiful recovery program. A person can start to move and make things happen in his life. The way he looks is different. The way he talks is different. The words he uses are different. He can say "I'm a cocaine addict," three times and be okay with it.

The Future

Cocaine addiction is a treatable disease from which victims can and do recover. There are, however, three troubling issues confronting everyone concerned with cocainism, the disease: the early age of onset of this addiction; the changing background and characteristics of the typical addict; and the reintegration of the addict back into the community after treatment.

Today everyone is concerned about crack and rock cocaine. For parents, afraid of the impact of this potent drug on the brain, age of onset of the disease is the troubling issue. Therapists and counselors are constantly hearing the question: "How can I get my son or my daughter off cocaine?" It's the toughest question in the world, and there's no simple answer. We know what must be done to recover from cocaine addiction but we cannot supply the willingness and desire for recovery. We don't have a formula to make these kids quit. We don't have a formula to make someone's husband or wife quit. I was once impressed by having a lady stand up during a seminar, as if no one else existed, and say, "My husband left me for cocaine. My life was just ideal a year ago, but today we owe fifty thousand dollars. We have to sell our car, our house . . . we're in hock up to our ears." She was jilted, jilted by the person she loved, for a white inert powder.

When we search for a solution to the cocaine problem we usually turn to supply. I wasn't sure whether to be angry or to laugh when I heard the President of Bolivia say that all we need is one hundred million dollars a year for the next four years, and maybe we can put a dent in this problem. You see, we are not going to stop supply unless we stop demand.

Urine testing and other maneuvers may be helpful, but while we have families that are dysfunctional, and role models who are chemically dependent or alcoholic–as long as we have people out there who are empty and who see cocaine as a missing piece–we will have demand for and a supply of the drug.

The profile of the cocaine addict is changing and this presents a whole new series of baffling problems for communities and treatment programs. 800-Cocaine described the typical cocaine addict of 1983 as college educated (50%), an intranasal user (61%), with a relatively low unemployment rate (16%) (considering the stage of the drug dependence progression), and earning over $25,000 per year. By 1988 this profile had shifted as shown in the table below. Herridge and Gold described statistically, in *Psyciatric Annals*, what many clinicians have informally concluded. The "new" cocaine addict is less educated and more likely to be an urban dweller than was the case in 1983. This usually means that the "new" cocaine addict will typically have fewer positive support systems. They also are much more likely to use the rapid delivery, highly addictive, freebase form of cocaine.

Table 1. Changing Characteristics of the Cocaine Addict

	1983	1988
College Educated	50%	16%
Freebase Use	21%	56%
Income 25K/Year	52%	20%

There are new treatment challenges arising from the change in demographic characteristics of the typical cocaine dependent. Can a black, urban freebaser enter a middle-class, blue-collar treatment program and have his needs met? Not if the treatment center says, "Just be like us–*Trust us–And surrender.*" New programs must be sensitive to ethnic and urban issues or this population will be ill-prepared for "recovery."

The third major recovery issue is the reintegration of the cocaine addict into the home, job and community. No matter how good and how dynamic our treatment approach, I have learned that the cocaine addict is extremely vulnerable to people, places, and things. When the environment they return to is one that reinforces the use of crack or rock cocaine, the potential for kinesthetic craving or "drug hunger" is overwhelming. When crack houses flourish, positive role models, alternative activities, strong self-help, half-way houses, and community based drop-in centers are typically, and tragically, absent.

Recovery and treatment are not the same. Recovery occurs over time, when an individual successfully reintegrates into the community, home, and job–when the addict discovers an easier, softer, way of life. Treatment only assists in the long-range process of recovery. The "new" cocaine addict may complete the initial treatment but relapse when structure and support are decreased.

How can treatment assist in successful reintegration? Here are several suggestions:

Develop strong volunteer networks. In areas where few positive role models exist and self-help is not well developed, former patients and persons in the recovering community can be mobilized to assist in the transition back into the community.

Phase down treatment. Many relapses occur when the patient walks out of a structured treatment unit with only one continuing care group per week as part of a professional aftercare plan. For example, phasing an inpatient setting into an intensive outpatient setting, or a half-way house, will increase support. Consider at least two continuing care meetings per week instead of just one. Phase down of intensity may also help the addict negotiate a "wall" that tends to occur some 60-85 days into recovery.

Transition patients into the next level of care early. For example, if the cocaine addict is leaving inpatient care, contact with the outpatient therapist should be initiated prior to graduation. During the last week of inpatient care the addict might meet with the continuing care group to establish comfort and bonding. A "buddy" system can easily be developed.

Liaison with the work place. When return to work is part of the discharge plan, a "helping person" on the job should be employed to assist in the reentry. Therapy groups and/or self-help meetings are possibilities. Employee assistance personnel can play a critical role in the reentry process.

Work with community leaders. In many communities mom and the church will be strong forces. Local leaders may also assist in helping to establish drop-in centers and positive alternatives to the street experience.

Keep it simple. My clinical experience with the urban crack addict leads me to believe that cognitive impairment is often present. Keep patient education simple and structured. Topics that concern understanding the disease, accepting addiction, and reintegration should be priorities.

A recent study summarized in the *Hazelden Professional Update* suggests that cocaine addicts are more impulsive than alcoholics when it comes to the reason for first use. Clinicians frequently observe cocaine addicts' inability to handle cravings and the intensity of these cravings. Proactive relapse strategies, as opposed to more reactive strategies, are necessary. Proactive strategies anticipate real life problems to be encountered upon reintegration and utilize treatment time to prepare for them. Preparation often includes changing old patterns. A People, Places and Things group may be much more beneficial to the cocaine addict than learning about THIQ's. Certainly, practical strategies, anticipating problems and changing old patterns, make better sense when we understand the need to negotiate the minefields (and mindfields) in the urban setting–an environment that promotes the sale of crack or rock.

It's a fast and easy way to make money. A person can make up to $150,000 just on a contract to use his private plane to fly a shipment of cocaine under radar. When you look at those sums of money, you see bankers and business people becoming involved. There was a big bust in Philadelphia, all lawyers and doctors and dentists who had been the principal suppliers of cocaine to the area since 1978. When you look at a bust of forty-six hundred pounds, and realize that cocaine is at least five times as valuable as gold, you begin to appreciate the magnitude of the cocaine economy.

What does this imply? You're an adolescent who wants to break out of a low socioeconomic area. You notice the person in your neighborhood who has the good clothes and expensive car–your role model, perhaps–and you look at the baseball players, and basketball and football players. When they are involved with cocaine, what will you conclude about how to succeed in life?

We've had ball players come out of treatment programs, and the next week they're on TV saying, "Kids, don't use drugs." And then, the following week, they are back in treatment, and then they are out playing. And this happens two or three times. They relapse, they play; they relapse, they play–and they make a million dollars a year. Now what do you conclude from that? The way to get what you want, the way to get out of this environment–the way to wealth and fame–the way to have the friends you want, and the way to material possessions is through the drug economy.

I'm thankful that someone told me that the value of baseball cards, of the players who were in the Peter Uberoth investigation for cocaine, has gone down in the eyes of our children. There is some hope. I think that political leaders, like Ronald and Nancy Reagan, making statements like "drugs are public enemy number one" is a positive act. We have some good role models coming out and saying, "Hey, there is a better way of life"–what self-help is calling the "easier, softer way of life"–a program where there is an intersection between our relationship with God and our relationship with our fellow man.

On many levels, a war to gain back communities from gangs and cocaine dealers is being waged. No national leaders, no toll-free numbers, and no direct mail solicitations support these local efforts. These efforts have few funds to match the money amassed by the illicit cocaine empire. Nevertheless, a powerful source of health and healing is our people and their capacity to love and care.

Cocaine addiction is a community problem, an *us* problem. Excellent treatment of addicts by dedicated professionals is not enough to solve it. Nor is law enforcement alone the answer. A genuine resolution of the crisis requires the involvement of the people–you and me. Niches of recovery must be established in our neighborhoods that model health and healing.

Even then, I don't think we will see zero cocaine use in our lifetimes. Human society has been on a six-thousand-year ride of drug and alcohol use. But at least we can plant an olive tree. Although it may not bear fruit in our lifetimes, it will bear fruit for our children and their children. Synergistically, the effects of education, treatment and society's emphasis on alternative behaviors to cocaine and other drug experiences can have a powerful, positive impact.

Cocaine addicts are not bad people. They are people with a disease; a disease manipulated, and whose victims are exploited, by an unscrupulous element in our society. This element offers a highly addictive and well-marketed product: *cocaine*. The price the addict pays for the ride is in the currency of disrupted families, lost jobs, lowered self-esteem, reduced freedom, and even life itself. Telling a cocaine addict to "Just say no!" doesn't work. It is like telling someone who is clinically depressed to "Have a good day!" What works is people understanding cocaine addiction, what treatment and alternative resources are available and, foremost, its people caring for people.

Consider this small miracle. It's early Sunday morning in an inner city community. A crack addict walks out onto the street after a cocaine binge. Out of money and drug, the addict is hurting and desperate. The addict asks someone standing on the street corner for help. Instead of offering more cocaine, this individual offers to take the addict to a treatment program or to a self-help meeting. Within this encounter lies the solution to our national crisis.

SCHEDULE C

A CLINICAL SELF-ASSESSMENT

(for Cocaine Dependence)

Cardwell C. Nuckols

Individual client assessment booklets can be purchased at low cost from Human Services Institute, P.O. Box 14610, Bradenton, Florida 34280.

Schedule C

A Clinical Self-Assessment (for Cocaine Dependence)

Schedule C provides a preliminary estimate of a cocaine user's current stage in the progression of cocaine dependence. The purpose of the assessment is to identify the physical and behavioral symptoms of cocaine use and to place these on a continuum.

Schedule C information gathering should be the clinician's first step in case assessment and therapy planning. The instrument was designed to enable a client to independently undertake a reliable self-assessment. Although it is ideal to elicit this information through in-depth case analysis, this is rarely practical. For example, cocaine users are likely to do a great deal of personal self-assessment, often unguided or misguided, before making a commitment to treatment. *Schedule C* helps answer the question, "Do I have a serious problem?"

If a clinician is already working with a cocaine addiction case, he or she can use *Schedule C* as a client rating schedule. If information on some of the items is lacking, it can be elicited directly or indirectly in clinical sessions. Using the schedule in this manner provides a broad, structured approach to understanding the dynamics of the case.

The written responses to *Schedule C* help expose the problem, causing the user to confront the realities of cocaine use. These responses help the cocaine user, the user's family and addiction professionals to see the exact nature and extent of the problem. It complements more extensive, professionally-administered evaluations. *Schedule C* is NOT an alternative to more in-depth clinical appraisals which are part of a treatment program.

The first part of the self-assessment schedule elicits an estimate of the degree or severity of the cocaine addiction. The model underlying *Schedule C* is that of a progressive disorder, consistent with the established medical definition wherein an addiction is viewed as having three major components:

Loss of Control

Compulsive Use

Continued Use Despite Adverse Consequences

The clinical approach to the treatment of addiction requires that the cocaine user be able to identify a progressive pattern of behaviors and that these behaviors be correlated with specific life problem areas.

The second part of the evaluation assesses life components or potential problem areas affected by cocaine. These are the areas where change is often necessary as part of a clinical treatment approach. The life components assessed are: Personal, Medical, Family and Friends, and Work and Finances.

Schedule C can be used in two ways. The client responds to the self-evaluation items and in doing so, achieves a detailed look at the problem. The client's responses, reviewed by a professional, serve as a guide for structuring the therapy and recovery program.

The Progression

Cocainism, a disease, is progressive. The progressive model of addiction encourages each person to identify and understand his or her own personal pattern of cocaine use. It is important to recognize and accept that the use of this drug is part of a progression which millions of other persons have experienced. Through these cases, we know what happens after each stage of addiction.

The progressive model presented here is unique to the cocaine addict. Alcoholism has a progression that has been termed the "Jellenick" model. The progress of cocaine addiction follows what I term the "DeLorean" model. The progression is divided into three separate stages. Each stage, from early to chronic, represents an increase in the severity of the illness.

The next pages describe behaviors that are indicators of the progression of cocaine addiction. The individual should darken the circles next to the behaviors that are part of his or her personal cocaine experience. Work from the top of the page to the bottom. Check all statements that apply to you. One assessment schedule is for a husband, wife or significant other, a boyfriend, girlfriend, brother, or sister who may have also used cocaine. It is crucial that they too cooperate in this assessment by examining their own cocaine use.

Following the schedules, illustrative case studies are provided. These case studies give examples to help a cocaine user begin to understand his or her own progression.

Early Stage

(Loss of Control)

Darken the circles before all the statements that apply to you.

O Use in a social situation (ex: at parties or with certain friends).

O Use only when others offer.

O Discovered that sex is heightened by cocaine use.

O Buy own cocaine.

O Watch the sunrise while using.

O Buy cocaine in larger quantities.

O Miss work or a social occasion because of use.

O Sell to close friends.

O Beginning to lose interest in other areas of life (ex: hobbies, certain people who don't use)

Middle Stage

(Compulsive Use)

O Hang around only with people who use cocaine.

O Only like social occasions where cocaine is present.

O Notice feeling suspicious of others.

O Once cocaine use starts, all available cocaine is consumed (or, if dealing, typically use 1/8 or 1/4 ounce at a sitting).

O Use alone or only with a few select persons.

O Social and/or work problems occurring weekly.

O Unable to perform sexually (women are non-orgasmic and men cannot maintain an erection).

Chronic Stage

(Continued Use Despite Adverse Consequences)

- O Work, financial and/or legal problems escalating.
- O Obsessed with the idea of obtaining more cocaine when original supply is gone.
- O Binge frequently, lasting twelve hours to days.
- O Experience almost constant depression when cocaine is unavailable.
- O Loss of weight, seizures, and/or chest pains.
- O Intense suspicion of others and hallucinations.
- O Experience feelings of helplessness and hopelessness regarding use.

Spouse or Significant Other

The spouse or significant other should darken the circles before the statements that apply to them.

- O Often feel suspicious.
- O Problems seem to be multiplying.
- O Daily arguments.
- O Often have feelings of distrust.
- O Use cocaine with spouse or loved one.
- O Use other drugs (alcohol, marijuana) with cocaine.
- O Use cocaine to enhance sexual relationship.
- O Family life disrupted.
- O Enjoys excitement of cocaine lifestyle.
- O Do things that cause guilt and shame.
- O Extreme depression.
- O Threats made but not carried out.
- O Loss of self-respect.

Life Components

This section helps the cocaine user identify the life components or personal areas threatened or damaged by cocaine use.

Life Components is divided into four parts:

Personal. How has cocaine affected you as a person?

Medical. How has your cocaine use affected your physical and mental condition?

Family & Friends. How has your cocaine use disturbed your family relations and friendships?

Work and Finance. How has your cocaine use affected your work and finances?

After completing this section and analyzing your level of addiction and life area problems, refer to the Recovery section for guidelines for using this data.

Just as in section one, darken the circles next to those behaviors that are a part of your own cocaine experience.

Personal

O Own cocaine paraphernalia (spoons, mirrors, pipes).
O Life is more enjoyable when using cocaine.
O After using cocaine, feel guilty and remorseful.
O Buy quantities of cocaine worth more than $100.
O Have tried to cut down on cocaine consumption.

O Have "cooked" freebase.
O Feel depressed between uses of cocaine.
O Experienced cocaine paranoia (strong suspicion of others).
O Have physically abused a friend or lover while using cocaine.
O Have used cocaine to enhance a sexual relationship.
O Have done things sexually I would not do while straight.
O Have had sexual affairs while using cocaine.
O Was abused sexually or physically as a child.

Feelings

Complete the following sentence:

"The feelings in life I cannot tolerate are..."

O Boredom
O Loneliness
O Tiredness
O Hunger
O Anger
O Happiness
O Fear (of being arrested for possessing and/or selling cocaine.)

Medical

Darken the circles before all the statements that apply to you.

O Lost weight since using cocaine. If so, how much?

- O 5-10 lbs.
- O 10-20 lbs.
- O More than 20 lbs.

- O Used depressant drugs like alcohol or Valium to "come down" from cocaine.
- O Used opiates like heroin, morphine, cocaine, Demerol or Percodan with cocaine.
- O Injected cocaine.
- O Thought about committing suicide while using or after using cocaine.
- O Had a self-destructive plan in mind.
- O Attempted suicide.
- O Experienced a seizure while using cocaine.
- O Experienced chest pains while using cocaine.
- O Had difficulty breathing while using cocaine.
- O Had sex with other drug users who injected drugs.
- O Had to go to a hospital emergency room due to cocaine use.

Do members of your family suffer from:

- O Alcoholism or drug dependency?
- O Depression?

Have you ever been told by a physician or psychologist that you suffer from:

- O Depression?
- O Alcoholism or drug dependence?
- O Other types of mental illness?

Family and Friends

Darken the circles before all the statements that apply to you.

- O Lied to family and/or friends because of cocaine use.
- O Argued with family and/or friends because of cocaine use.
- O Began to avoid old friends who don't use cocaine in favor of new friends who do use.
- O Used cocaine with spouse or boyfriend/girlfriend.
- O Become resentful when friends have more cocaine.
- O Sought friendships with people who have more money for, or better access to, cocaine.
- O Developed relationships with people I normally would not, due to cocaine.
- O Been threatened with divorce, separation, or loss of boyfriend/girlfriend due to cocaine use.
- O Used family members to help get or sell cocaine.
- O Alcoholism or drug dependence exists in immediate family (mother, father, sister, brother, grandparent).

Work and Finances

Darken the circles before all the statements that apply to you.

- O Missed work due to cocaine.
- O Taken sick days due to cocaine.
- O Used cocaine while at work.
- O Purchased cocaine FROM people at work.
- O Purchased cocaine FOR people at work.
- O Work with people who often have cocaine.
- O Been suspended or threatened with disciplinary action due to cocaine use.
- O Borrowed money to purchase cocaine or pay cocaine debts.
- O Had cocaine "fronted" and could not afford to pay back debt due to over-consumption of cocaine.

- O Been "threatened" by someone owed money.
- O "Threatened" someone else who owed me money.
- O Became dependent on money received from selling cocaine to maintain current lifestyle.
- O Thought about making more money or getting a promotion in order to purchase more cocaine.

Case Study #1 - Progression

Mary S. is a twenty-four-year-old female. She had been snorting cocaine for the past eighteen months and was concerned about its high cost and the growing importance it was having in her life. Mary checked the following behaviors that related to her:

Early Stage Indicators

- ✓ Used in a social situation.
- ✓ Discovered that sex was heightened by cocaine use.
- ✓ Buys own cocaine.
- ✓ Watches the sunrise while using.
- ✓ Sells to close friends.
- ✓ Started to lose interest in other areas of life.

Middle Stage Indicators

- ✓ Only likes social occasions where cocaine is present.

In assessing her behaviors, all except "only likes social occasions where cocaine is present" (middle stage behavior) are early stage symptoms. These symptoms reveal that Mary is progressively losing control of her use and is entering the second or middle stage of cocaine addiction. The middle stage is marked by progressive preoccupation with cocaine and its compulsive use. If Mary continues to use cocaine we will see her lose further control and develop more self, social, and occupational symptoms of the disease of cocainism. Mary is not currently involved in a relationship. Therefore, no assessment was done by spouse or significant other.

Life Progression

Mary S. is entering the middle stage of her illness. The major sign is progressive loss of control and compulsive use. In assessing life components, Mary checked many behaviors that are indicative of problems in her personal life and with family and friends.

Personal

- ✓ Owns cocaine paraphernalia (spoons, mirrors, pipes, etc.).
- ✓ Feels guilty and remorseful after using cocaine.
- ✓ Buys quantities of cocaine worth more than $100.
- ✓ Has tried to cut down on cocaine consumption.
- ✓ Feels depressed between uses of cocaine.
- ✓ Was physically abused by a lover while using cocaine.
- ✓ Used cocaine to enhance a sexual relationship.
- ✓ Has sexual affairs while using cocaine.
- ✓ Was abused sexually as a child.

Family & Friends

- ✓ Lied to her family because of cocaine use.
- ✓ Argued with her family because of cocaine use.
- ✓ Resentful of friends who have more cocaine.
- ✓ Sought friendships with people who have better access to cocaine.
- ✓ Alcoholism exists in immediate family.

In combining both the progression with problems in life components, the impression of Mary S. is that she is entering the middle stage of her cocaine addiction. Her recovery plan must address areas in her personal and family life.

Case Study #2 - Progression

Matthew J. is a thirty-one-year-old male who has a long history of substance and alcohol abuse dating back to his adolescent years. He comes from a home where his father is an alcoholic. When he first came to the clinic he had been "busted" for possession with intent to distribute. Matthew checked the following behaviors about himself:

Early Stage Indicators

- ✓ Discovered that sex is heightened by cocaine use.
- ✓ Buys own cocaine.
- ✓ Watches the sunrise while using.
- ✓ Buys cocaine in larger quantities.
- ✓ Misses work or social occasions because of use.
- ✓ Sells to close friends.
- ✓ Started to lose interest in other areas of life.
- ✓ Started to hang around only with people who use cocaine.

Middle Stage Indicators

- ✓ Notice feeling suspicious of others.
- ✓ Once use starts, all available cocaine is consumed.
- ✓ Uses alone or only with a few select persons.
- ✓ Social and/or work problems occurring frequently.

Chronic Stage Indicators

- ✓ Is obsessed with the idea of obtaining more cocaine when original supply is gone.
- ✓ Binges frequently lasting twelve hours to days.

In assessing Matthew's behavior, it is clear that he has progressed through both the early and middle stages of cocaine addiction. He is displaying symptoms of the chronic stage of cocainism. Matthew's behavior shows continued use of cocaine despite mounting problems and damage to his personal life. Sally, Matthew's wife, checked the following behaviors:

- ✓ Daily Arguments.
- ✓ Distrust.
- ✓ Using cocaine together.
- ✓ Using cocaine to enhance sexual relationship.

Sally needs further assessment to determine her own progression.

Life Progression

Matthew J. has progressed through both the early and middle stages of his cocaine addiction. He is currently in the chronic stage, characterized by continued use despite adverse consequences. Matthew's situation is further complicated by his wife Sally's use of cocaine. In assessing life components, all areas revealed problems (Personal, Medical, Family and Friends, and Work and Finances).

Personal

- ✓ Owns cocaine paraphernalia (spoons, mirrors, pipes, etc.).
- ✓ Life has more enjoyment when using cocaine.
- ✓ Feels guilty or remorseful after using.

- ✓ Buys quantities of cocaine worth more than $100.
- ✓ Cooked freebase cocaine.
- ✓ Experienced cocaine paranoia.
- ✓ Acted out sexually while using cocaine.
- ✓ Cannot tolerate feelings of boredom and fear of arrest.

Medical

- ✓ Lost 15 pounds since using cocaine.
- ✓ Injected cocaine.
- ✓ Thought about committing suicide after using cocaine.
- ✓ Experienced a seizure while using cocaine.
- ✓ Had sex with other drug users who injected drugs.
- ✓ Had to go to a hospital emergency room due to cocaine use.

Family and Friends

- ✓ Avoided old friends in favor of new friends who use cocaine.
- ✓ Used cocaine with girlfriend.
- ✓ Sought friendships for better access to cocaine.
- ✓ Threatened with loss of girlfriend due to cocaine use.
- ✓ Brother is drug dependent.

Work and Finances

- ✓ Misses work due to cocaine.
- ✓ Taken sick days due to cocaine.
- ✓ Used cocaine while at work.
- ✓ Purchased cocaine FOR people at work.
- ✓ Borrowed money to purchase cocaine.
- ✓ Been "threatened" by someone you owe money.

In combining both the progression and problems in life components, the impression of Matthew J. is that he is in the chronic stage of his cocaine addiction. He has problems in all areas of life. The situation is complicated by the fact that his wife Sally may also be cocaine dependent.

Recovery

If there is evidence of cocaine addiction, what should I do about it? First, results from this self-assessment should be discussed with an addiction professional or someone who is familiar with drug addiction. Many treatment programs offer free and confidential consultation. Self-help groups such as Narcotics Anonymous and Cocaine Anonymous can help create an action plan that may lead to recovery.

Treatment is available at many levels of intensity. The least restrictive is outpatient and the most intensive is either intensive outpatient or inpatient treatment. The following represent some rules-of-thumb for choosing a treatment:

1. The further you have progressed in the addiction, the more intense the treatment required.

2. The more life components affected, the more intense the treatment required.

3. The presence of medical, psychological, or past out-patient failures demand inpatient remedies.

4. In the absence of good external support systems (i.e., family, job, friends, etc.)

consideration should be given to more intensive treatment.

It is important to discuss your situation with an addiction specialist (doctor, drug counselor or psychologist) or a person who is achieving a personal recovery.

Always remember: There is hope. Recovery is within reach.

Appendix B

"Controlled Substances Act"
Comprehensive Drug Abuse Prevention and Control Act of 1970

P.L. 91-513

An Overview of Legal Aspects

In 1970, the United States federal government enacted the Controlled Substances Act which established five categories or "schedules" listing potentially abused medications.

SCHEDULE I:

Highest potential for abuse with no recognized medical use (except for experimental purposes).

Example - Heroin, LSD, Marijuana, and Pep

Penalties - First offense penalties for trafficking in Schedule I drugs range from 5-15 years with a $15,000-$25,000 fine

SCHEDULE II:

High potential for abuse but have legitimate medical uses.

Example - Barbiturates, Amphetamines, Cocaine, and narcotics (Morphine, Demerol, etc.)

Penalties- Same as Schedule I

SCHEDULE III:

Moderate potential for abuse (low to moderate potential for physical dependence or high potential for psychological dependence); with legitimate medical uses.

Example - Nonamphetamine type stimulants and nonbariturate sedatives (Quaaludes are Schedule II)

Penalties - Trafficking involves a 5-year sentence and a $15,000 fine for first offense

SCHEDULE IV:

Low abuse potential with limited likelihood of creating physical or psychological dependence.

Example - Darvon; some sedatives and pain killers that do not contain narcotics

Penalties - Trafficking involves 3-year sentence and $10,000 fine

SCHEDULE V:

Low potential for abuse and may lead to limited physical or psychological dependence.

Example - Drugs containing small amounts of narcotics and are used for cough and diarrhea

Penalties - Trafficking penalties are one year and a $5,000 fine

Glossary

Acceptance: Often called surrender in self-help groups, this term is the opposite of willpower. Acceptance means willingness to admit that our life is out of control, and that we need the help of a higher power (some power outside of ourselves) to lead us from the insanity of drug or alcohol addiction. See Willpower.

Addiction: Loss of control of the intake of alcohol or drugs with continued use despite adverse consequences.

Addictionologist: Medical term for a specialist in the treatment of addictionology.

Adult Children: Those who encountered developmental difficulties growing up in an alcoholic or chemically dependent family.

Adulterant: See Cut.

Alcoholics Anonymous (AA): A fellowship of men and women who share their hopes, strengths and experiences such that they help each other in recovery. AA is a support group primarily for alcoholics and is not to be confused with professional treatment.

Amphetamine: A central nervous system stimulant with sympathomimetic effects; common ingredient in prescription diet pills used in the 60's and 70's. Cocaine is pharmacologically very similar to amphetamines.

Amphetamine Psychosis: A condition sometimes occuring among amphetamine users, typically after high dose. Consists of delirium, hallucinations and persecutory delusions.

Anchored Experience: A past experience that can be triggered by being in a similar set or setting. See Internal and External Cues.

Anchors: See Internal and External Cues.

Anhedonia: Inability to feel pleasure; a common symptom of Parkinson's disease.

Arrhythmia: An irregular rhythm, often describing heart problem (i.e., cardiac arrhythmia).

Aversive Conditioning: A psychological term for associating a former pleasurable experience, like using cocaine, with a negative consequence.

Benzodiazepines: A pharmacological class of tranquilizing drugs; examples include Valium, Librium, and Xanax.

Blow: A street name for cocaine.

Bust: To be "busted" or caught for possession or distribution of an illegal substance.

Carbacaine: An anesthetic used in medicine that has a "freeze" similar to cocaine. It can be used as an adulterant or "cut."

Cocaine: A central nervous system stimulant with profound sympathomimetic effects; it can be insufflated (snorted), given intravenously (injected), or inhaled through the lungs (free based). See Cocaine HC1, Freebase, I.N. and I.V.

Cocaine Anonymous (CA): A new fellowship, comprised of persons addicted to cocaine, that follows the 12-step program of Alcoholics Anonymous.

Cocaine Bugs: A true halluciation first described in 1889 in Paris, France by Dr. Magnan. Also called Magnan's sign, formication, or parasitosis. Usually seen in high dose chronic uses, the user believes there are bugs under the skin. See True Hallucination.

Cocaine HC1: When the alkaloid cocaine is mixed with an acid (HC1) the product yielded is cocaine HC1, the highly water soluble compound used for insufflation (snorting) or intravenous (I.V.) administration.

Cocaine Psychosis: Typically reversible psychiatric condition characterized by loss of reality. In extreme cases it can mimic paranoid schizophrenia. See Paranoid Schizophrenic.

Contingency Contracting: A contract with a recovering addict where a negative or positive consequence is attached to the addict's fulfillment of agreed upon stipulations.

Copping: Procuring a drug for consumption, in this case cocaine.

Coming Down: When the blood levels of cocaine are decreasing and the user starts to experience what is often described as "anguish."

Crack: Term describing the sound that cocaine makes when it is smoked or freebased.

Crank: A term that often means a state of stimulation of the brain, as in "cranked up" or "wired."

Cravings: Also called drug hunger, a desire to use a drug such as cocaine often in order to alleviate subjective distress.

Cut: Substance added to cocaine to increase volume and weight and to increase profitability. The two typical types of cut include: 1) Inert sugars - Example: inositol, added to increase volume and weight; 2) Other anesthetics - Example: lidocaine, added to give the characteristic anesthetic 'freeze,' in addition to increasing volume and weight.

Cyclothymic Disorder: A disorder of affect or mood involving periods of depression or hypomania.

D.T.s: Delirium Tremens.

Denial: A psychological defense system used to help an individual disavow reality.

Dependence: Used interchangeably with addiction. See Addiction.

Disassociating: Acting as if one were a spectator to one's own subjective experience, allowing one to be more objective about an emotional experience.

Dopamine: A neurotransmitter or brain chemical involved in both the pleasurable experience of the cocaine high and the dysphoria of "coming off" of it.

Drug-a-logues: The telling of drug related stories. This typically happens in early recovery when addicts have very little recovery history to discuss.

Dual Diagnosis: Category describing an individual with two disorders. In the context of this book it refers to a diagnosis of chemical dependency along with an existing psychiatric diagnosis (Example: depression).

Dysphoria: Feeling bad.

Dysphoric Rebound: After a euphoric mood a person may have an alternating effect of dysphoria as the blood level of cocaine diminishes.

Edge: Refers to side effects such as tight muscles and grinding teeth, which detract from the euphoric experience.

Eight-ball: Street term for an eighth of an ounce of cocaine.

Electroencephalogram: A measurement of brain wave activity.

Euphoric Recall: The kinesthetic (emotional) recall of the positive aspects of drug use. May be accompanied by physiological signs such as increased heart rate and perspiration.

External Cues: A part of the total drug experience (see Total Drug Experience), incorporating the setting or environmental influences upon the individual. AA often refers to the External People, Places and Things.

Freebase: A smokeable form of cocaine.

Freebasing: The act of smoking cocaine whereby vapors are inahled directly into the lungs. This is the most rapid way of getting cocaine into the system.

Freeze: An anesthetic or numbing effect.

Haldol: An antipsychotic medication.

Hallucinations: Seeing, hearing or feeling things that in fact do not exist.

Head Magazine: Magazine that contains advertisements for drug related paraphernalia, typically for mail order.

Hit: A unit dose of cocaine. Can be a "line" of cocaine for snorting, a syringeful of cocaine for injecting, or a "rock" of cocaine for freebasing.

Hotshot: An injection of a drug other than the drug expected, or an injection where the purity is greater than that expected.

Hyperkinesia: A disorder with inappropriate degrees of attention, impulsiveness and hyperactivity; an attention deficit disorder.

Hyperpyrexia: Elevated, above normal body temperature. The cocaine addict's body temperatures may escalate as high as 107 to 108 degrees. If not properly controlled, over time this can be lethal.

Hypersomnia: A lethargic, sleepy-state often found in early abstinence from cocaine.

I.N.: See Intranasal.

Intranasal (I.N.): The intranasal use of cocaine, by insufflation or "snorting" of cocaine into the nose for absorption by the nasal membranes.

Inositol: A popular inert "cut" added to increase weight and volume–and profits.

Inpatient: A treatment setting where patients live 24-hours a day in a hospital or residential unit.

Inpatient Rehabilitation: Professionally regulated treatment usually lasting three to four weeks. May be hospital or residential-based.

Insufflation: The inhaling through the nostrils of cocaine; also called "snorting."

Intensive Outpatient Program: A program designed to clinically supply the treatment modalities found in a more restrictive inpatient environment, minus the supportive milieu.

Internal Cues: A part of the total drug experience; cues incorporating the "set" or psychological make-up of the individual, psychological make-up being influenced by past experience and expectation. See Total Drug Experience.

Intravenous (I.V.): Intravenously using cociane, i.e., injecting cocaine in solution into the venous system.

I.V.: See Intravenous.

Kindling: A type of reverse tolerance to cocaine. Overdose phenomena–like seizures–are experienced at a lower dose than typically tolerated.

Kinky: Unusual or bizarre (as in the sexual practice of bondage under the influence of cocaine).

Lidocaine: A popular cocaine "cut" that has the characteristic numbing and freezing sensation of cocaine. See Cut.

Lithium: A prescribed medication often used to treat bi-polar illness, or manic depression.

Manic-depressive: A psychiatric condition characterized by depressive and manic mood sweeps, more correctly called bi-polar disorder.

Matures Out: A tendency to quit a certain activity with age. Many heroin addicts "mature out" of their use of heroin in their mid-to-late thirties.

Meta-message: The true message.

Monito: A baby laxative that looks just like cocaine and is often used as a "cut" or adulterant. See Cut.

Motivational Crisis: A crisis that escalates pain levels in the cocaine addict such that treatment may be considered an alternative or an imperative. This crisis is often financial or legal.

Nanogram: A very small unit of measure; 1/1000 of a gram.

Nanogram Percent: The number of nanograms of a substance found in 100 ml of blood.

Narcissism: In this context we are referring to "specialness" or "uniqueness" that is part of the cocaine addict's self-perception in early treatment.

Narcissistic Personality Disorder: When narcissistic tendencies are exaggerated and cause problems with the individual's ability to function. Refer to the Diagnostic and Statistical Manual III of the American Psychiatric Association.

Narcotics Anonymous (NA): A self-help organization that provides support for recovering drug addicts.

Narcs: Narcotics police officers working undercover.

Neurotransmitters: Chemicals found in the brain and body that are responsible for the continuing transmission of nerve impulses.

Norepinephrine: A stimulatory neurotransmitter, also called Noradrenaline. See Neurotransmitters.

Nuking (the cocaine): The use of a microwave oven as a heat catalyst for the conversion of cocaine HC1 into freebase.

Ounce: A unit dose of cocaine, made up of 28 grams.

Outpatient Treatment: Typically involves the patient living at home while attending treatment services. Outpatient services have varying degrees of service intensity. See Intensive Outpatient Program.

Outpatient Therapy: Professional therapy provided on a least restrictive basis such that client or patient lives at home and utilizes a treatment center one or more times per week.

Parallel Treatment: A treatment strategy used when two disorders occur within one individual, which incorporates the belief that both disorders must be treated somewhat simultaneously, instead of one at a time. See Dual Diagnosis.

Paranoia: A psychological state that may involve a person perceiving that others are out to harm him.

Paranoid Schizophrenic: A psychiatric condition characterized by paranoia in conjunction with a thought and emotional disorder; can lead to violent action.

PCP: Phencylidine, a mood altering illegal drug; sometimes mixed with freebase (space base).

pH: The degree of alkalinity or acidity of the body fluids.

Placebo Effect: Experience of a drug's effect (pain-killing, euphoria-producing, etc.) in a situation where the person believes he is taking a powerful drug but, in reality, is not.

Polydrug: Meaning more than one drug; term typically used to describe a user of more than one type of psychoactive substance, either concurrently or sequentially.

Procaine: An anesthetic sometimes used to "cut" or adulterate cocaine. See Cut.

Professional Treatment: Describes a professionally regulated therapy, such as inpatient rehabilitation or outpatient therapy.

Pseudo-hallucination: When people perceive sensations (auditory, visual, or kinesthetic) which they know, intellectually, do not exist. See Snow Lights.

Quaaludes: A hypnotic or sleep-producing drug. Although removed from the U.S. market, may still be obtained illegally.

Reefer: Marijuana.

Relapse: A return to the use of alcohol and/or drugs; also refers to a process in early recovery where a patient builds up to the use of alcohol or a drug.

Remote Ideation: A vague idea, as opposed to an immediate well-defined plan.

Reverse Rituals: Reversing the old drug-related rituals (i.e., instead of using the pipe to smoke cocaine, taking the pipe and ceremoniously destroying it).

Rock: Term describing the appearance of cocaine which is to be smoked or freebased.

Running Set: Persons of similar drug-using habits making up the addict's social support system.

Rush: The experience of "getting off" on a drug; a time when there is an escalating blood level of a drug, experienced by the user as pleasurable.

Score: To "cop" or procure a drug.

Seizure: An electrical overreaction of the brain that can be caused by toxic doses of the powerful brain stimulant cocaine.

Self-Help: Describes any of the supportive type of fellowships such as Alcoholics Anonymous (AA), Narcotics Anonymous (NA), or Cocaine Anonymous (CA).

Serotonin: A neurotransmitter involved in sleep and mood control; it is depleted by chronic cocaine use.

Set, Setting: See Internal Cues.

Shake and Bake: A street method for converting cocaine HC1 into freebase.

Shoot: To inject a drug directly into a vein.

Slab: Term used for crack and rock or freebase. Instead of being a one-unit dose, the slab is a multiple dose amount in one chunk.

Snorting: See Insufflation.

Snow: Another colloquial or "street" term for cocaine.

Snow Lights: A pseudo-hallucination often described by chronic cocaine addicts as silver or white specks or geometric forms, typically seen in the peripheral visual field. See Pseudo-hallucination.

Space Base: The combination of PCP with freebase. See PCP and Freebase.

Speedball: The combination of cocaine with heroin; typically injected but may be combined and smoked.

Sponsor: Former addict who is capable of helping a newly recovering addict via support, advice, and modeling.

Stash: An amount of cocaine intended for the personal use of the consumer, and not meant for resale (often referred to as a "personal stash").

Status Epilepticus: A medical condition where there is not one isolated seizure, but life-threatening repeated seizures.

Strobing: A condition caused by high-dose cocaine administration where there is a flickering of the visual images perceived by the eye.

Sublimation: Substitution.

Sympathomimetic: Cocaine's ability to mimic the effects of the sympathetic nervous system, or the "fight or flight" nervous system. See Amphetamine and Cocaine.

Thorazine: An anti-psychotic prescription medication.

Titrate: The mixing of combinations of mood-altering substances to establish a desired effect.

Toot: Another term for cocaine, often used in reference to snorting or insufflation of cocaine.

Torch: To light or to heat with a match or other source of fire.

Total Drug Experience (TDE): An individual's subjective experience when consuming a mind-altering substance. TDE incorporates the direct pharmacologic effect with the internal and external cues. See Internal and External Cues.

Tricyclic Anti-Depressant: A prescription medication used to treat depression.

Tryptophan: An essential or necessary amino acid often used in treatment of cocaine addiction to restore depleted Serotonin.

True Hallucination: When the individual perceives sensations (auditory, visual, kinesthetic) that are believed to be real.

Tyrosine: An amino acid which may be used to expedite the replacement of neurochemical deficits during early recovery.

Unit Dose: One dose.

Vena Cava: The large vein entering the right side of the heart.

Willpower: The belief that, "If I were strong enough and tough enough, I 'should . . . could . . . can . . . ' deal with this drug or alcohol problem by myself." Opposite of surrender or acceptance. See Acceptance.

Wired: Suffering from the grating side effects of stimulant drugs like cocaine and amphetamines.

Bibliography

Articles

Acker, D., *et al.* "Abruptio placentae associated with cocaine use." *Am J Obstet Gynecol* 146 (May 1983):220-221.

"Adverse effects of cocaine abuse." *Med Lett Drugs Ther* 26 (May 25, 1984):51-52.

Anderson, K. "Crashing on Cocaine." *Time* (Apr 11, 1983):22-31.

Anker, A. L., *et al.* "Use of contingency contracts in speciality clinics for cocaine abuse." *Natl Inst Drug Abuse Res Monogr Ser* 41 (April 1982):452-459.

Bar-Or, D., *et al.* "Cocaine intoxication, delirium, death in body packer," [letter] *Ann Emerg Med* 11 (July 1982):389-390.

Barash, P. G., *et al.* "Is cocaine a sympathetic stimulant during general anesthesia?" *JAMA* 243 (April 1989):1437-1439.

Barrett, J. E. "Effects of alcohol, chlordiazepoxide, cocaine and pentobarbital on responding maintained under fixed-interval schedules of food or shock presentation." *J Pharmacol Exp Ther* 196 (March 1976):605-615.

Barton, R. P., *et al.* "The transport of crystalline cocaine in the nasal mucous blanket." *J Laryngol Otol* 93 (December 1979): 1191-1194.

Baselt, R. C. "Stability of cocaine in biological fluids." J Chromatogr 268 (October 1983):502-505.

Baxter, L. R. "Desipramine in the treatment of hypersomnolence following abrupt cessation of cocaine use." *Am J Psychiatry* 140 (November 1983):1525-1526.

Benchimol, A., *et al*. "Accelerated ventricular rhythm and cocaine abuse." *Ann Intern Med* 88 (April 1978):519-520.

Bettinger, J. "Cocaine intoxication: massive oral overdose." *Ann Emerg Med* 9 (August 1989):429-430.

Brady, J. V., *et al*. "Behavioral procedures for evaluating the relative abuse potential of CNS drugs in primates." *Fed Proc* 35 (September 1976):2245-2253.

Brady, J. V., *et al*. "Drug-maintained performance and the analysis of stimulant reinforcing effects." 599-610. In: Ellinwood, E. H., Jr., and M. M. Kilbey, ed. *Cocaine and Other Stimulants.* New York: Plenum Press, 1977.

"The Brompton cocktail." [editorial] *Lancet* 1 (June 9, 1979: 1220-1221.

Budd, R. D. "Cocaine radioimmunoassay-structure versus reactivity." *Clin Toxicol* 18 (July 1981):773-782.

Byck, R., *et al*. "Cocaine: blood concentration and physiological effect after intranasal application in man." 629-645. In: Byck, R., *et al*. "What are the Effects of Cocaine in Man?" *Natl Inst Drug Abuse Res Monogr* Series 13 (May, 1977):97-117.

Caffrey, R. J. "Counter-attack on cocaine trafficking: the strategy of drug law enforcement." *Bull Narc* 36 (April-June 1984): 57-63.

Caruana, D. S., *et al*. "Cocaine-packet ingestion. Diagnosis, management, and natural history." *Ann Intern Med* 100 (January 1984):73-74.

Castellani, S. A., *et al*. "Tolerance to cocaine-induced convulsions in the cat." *Eur J Pharmacol* 47 (January 1978):57-61.

Catravas, J. D., *et al*. "Antidotes for cocaine poisoning." [letter] *N Engl J Med* 297 (December 1977):1238.

Chasnoff, I. J., *et al*. "Cocaine use in pregnancy." *N Engl J Med* 313 (September 1985):666-669.

Chinn, D. M., *et al.* "Gas chromatography-chemical ionization mass spectrometry of cocaine and its metabolites in biological fluids." *J Anal Toxicol* 4 (January-February 1980):37-42.

Chitwood, D. D., *et al.* "Factors which differentiate cocaine users in treatment from nontreatment users." *Int J Addict* 20 (March 1985):449-459.

Clark, C. C. "Gas-liquid chromatographic quantitation of cocaine. HCI in powders and tablets: collaborative study." *J Assoc Off Anal Chem* 61 (May 1978):683-686.

____ "Mass spectral quantitation of cocaine HCI in powders." *J Assoc Off Anal Chem* 64 (July 1981):884-888.

"Cocaine." *Med Lett Drugs Ther* 21 (February 23, 1979):18-19.

"Cocaine fatalities". *New York Medical Journal* 55 (1982):457.

"Cocaine 'snorting' for fun." [editorial] *Med J Aust* 2 (July 10, 1976):40.

Cohen, S. "Cocaine." *JAMA* 231 (January 1975):74-75.

____ "Recent developments in the abuse of cocaine." *Bull Narc* 36 (April-June 1984):3-14.

Colp, R., Jr. "Notes on Dr. William S. Halsted." *Bull NY Acad Med* 60 (November 1984):876-887.

Colpaert, F. C., *et al.* "Cocaine cue in rats as it relates to subjective drug effects: a preliminary report." *Eur J Pharmacol* 40 (November 1976):195-199.

____ "Factors regulating drug cue sensitivity: Limits of discriminability and the role of a progressively decreasing training dose in cocaine-saline discrimination." *Neuropharmacology* 21 (November 1982):1187-1194.

Crowley, T. J. "Cautionary note on methylphenidate for cocaine dependence." [letter] *Am J Psychiatry* 141 (February 1984): 327-328.

D'Mello, G., *et al.* "Cocaine and amphetamine as discriminative stimuli in rats." [proceedings] *Br J Pharmacol* 59 (March 1977): 453-454.

____ "Interaction of cocaine with chlordiazepoxide assessed by motor activity in mice." *Br J Pharmacol* 59 (January 1977): 151-155.

Dackis, C. A. and M. S. Gold. "Bromocriptine as a treatment for cocaine abuse." [letter] *Lancet* (May 18, 1985):1151-1152.

____ "Pharmacological approaches to cocaine addiction." *J Substance Abuse Treatment* 2 (December 1985):139-145.

De Vito, J. J. "Cocaine intoxication." *Med Times* 103 (October 1975):189.

De Wit, H. and R. A. Wise. "Blockade of cocaine reinforcement in rats with the dopamine receptor blocker pimozide, but not with the noradrenergic blockers phentolamine or phenoxybenzamine." *Can J Psychol* 31 (December 1977):195-203.

Dehpour, A. R., *et al*. "Effect of denervation and cocaine on the response of isolated rat vas deferens to noradrenaline and methoxamine." [proceedings] *Br J Pharmacol* 58 (October 1976):280.

Dipalma, J. R. "Cocaine abuse and toxicity." *Am Fam Physician* 24 (November 1981):236-238.

Dougherty, J., *et al*. "Effects of phenobarbital and SKF 525A on cocaine self-administration in rats." pp. 135-43. In: Singh, J. M. and H. Lal (ed.). "Drug addiction." Vol.3: *Neurobiology and influences on behavior*. New York: Stratton, 1974.

Egan, D. J., *et al*. "Cocaine: recreational drug of choice?" *Rocky Mt Med J* 75 (January-February 1978):34-36.

Ehrlich, P., *et al*. "Cocaine recovery support groups and the language of recovery." *J Psychoactive Drugs* 17 (January-March 1985):11-17.

Einstein, S. *The Use and Misuse of Drugs*. Belmont, CA: Wadsworth Publishing, 1970.

Eiswirth, N. A., *et al*. "Cocaine: Champagne of Uppers." *Uppers and Downers*. Englewood Cliffs, NJ: Prentice-Hall, 1973.

Ellinwood, E. H. "Amphetamine and cocaine." pp. 467-476. In: M. E. Jarvik (ed.). *Psychopharmacology in the practice of medicine.* New York: Appleton-Century-Crofts, 1977.

Ellinwood, E., *et al*. "Stimulant abuse in man. The use of animal models to assess and predict behavioral toxicity." pp. 81-123. In: Thompson T. and K. R. Unna (ed.). *Predicting dependence liability of stimulant and depressant drugs.* Baltimore: Univ Park Press, 1977.

Emmett-Oglesby, M. W., *et al*. "Discriminative stimulus properties of a small dose of cocaine." *Neuropharmacology* 22 (January 1983):97-101

Ensing, J. G. "Bazooka: Cocaine-base and manganese carbonate." [letter] *J Anal Toxicol* 9 (January-February, 1985):45-46.

Eskes, D. "Thin-layer chromatographic procedure for the differentiation of the optical isomers of cocaine." *J Chromatogr* 152 (May 1978):589-591.

Esposito, R. U., *et al.* "Cocaine: acute effects on reinforcement thresholds for self-stimulation behavior to the medial forebrain bundle." *Pharmacol Biochem Behav* 8 (April 1978):437-439.

Fainsinger, M. H. "Unusual foreign bodies in bowel." *JAMA* 237 (May 1977):2225-2226.

Fischman, M. W., *et al.* "Cocaine self-administration in humans." *Fed Proc* 41 (February 1982):241-246.

Fischman, M. W., *et al.* "Physiological and behavioral effects of intravenous cocaine in man." pp. 647-64. In: Ellinwood, E. H., Jr., and M. M. Kilbey (ed.). *Cocaine and other stimulants*. New York: Plenum Press, 1977.

Fishbain, D. A., *et al.* "Cocaine intoxication, delirium, and death in a body packer." *Ann Emerg Med* 10 (October 1981): 531-532.

Freed, T. A., *et al.* "Case reports balloon obturation bowel obstruction: a hazard of drug smuggling." *Am J Rosentgenol* 127 (December 1976):1033-1034.

Friedman, M. "Cocaine mud." [letter] *JAMA* 239 (March 1978): 929.

Gawin, F. H. and Herbert D. Kleber, M.D.. "Cocaine abuse treatment: Open pilot trial with desipramine and lithium carbonate." *Arch Gen Psychiatry* 41 (September 1984):903-909.

Gay, G. R. "Clinical management of acute and chronic cocaine poisoning." *Ann Emerg Med* 11 (October 1982):562-72.

_____ "Propranolol combats cocaine effects." [letter] *JACEP* 5 (July 1976):549.

Gay, G. R., *et al.* "An' ho, ho, baby, take a whiff on me." La Dama Blanca cocaine in current perspective. Cleveland: *Anesth Analg* 55 (July-August 1976):582-587.

_____ "Cocaine: history, epidemiology, human pharmacology, and treatment. A perspective on a new debut for an old girl." *Clin Toxicol* 8(2) (1975):149-78.

Gilbert, E. F., *et al*. "The effects of cocaine in the production of cardiovascular anomalies in beta-adrenoreceptor stimulated chick embryos." *Experientia* 32 (August 1976):1026-1027.

Ginzburg, H. M. "Intravenous drug users and the acquired immune deficiency syndrome." *Public Health Rep* 99 (March-April, 1984):206-12.

Gold, M. S., *et al*. "New insights and treatments: opiate withdrawal and cocaine addiction." *Clin Ther* 7(1) (1984):6-21.

_____ "Cocaine withdrawal: Efficacy of tyrosine." Paper presented at the 13th annual meeting of the Society for Neuroscience, Boston, Nov 6-11, 1983.

Goldberg, M. F. "Cocaine: the first local anesthetic and the third scourge of humanity. A centennial melodrama." *Arch Ophthalmol* 102 (October 1984):1443-1447.

Goldberg, S. R., *et al*. "Reinforcement of behavior by cocaine injections." pp. 523-544. In: Ellinwood, E. H., Jr., and M. M. Kilbey (ed.). *Cocaine and other stimulants*. New York: Plenum Press, 1977.

Goldberg, S. T., *et al*. "Behavior controlled by scheduled injections of cocaine in squirrel and rhesus monkeys." *J Exp Anal Behav* 25 (January 1976):93-104.

Gorelick, P. B., *et al*. "Corning, cocaine and local anesthesia." [letter] *Arch Ophthalmol* 103 (March 1985):325.

Gould, L. C, *et al*. "Changing patterns of multiple drug use among applicants to a multimodality drug treatment program." *Arch Gen Psychiatry* 31 (September 1974):408-13.

Grabowski, John (ed.). "Cocaine: Pharmacology, Effects and Treatment of Abuse." Rockville, MD: *National Institute on Drug Abuse Research Monograph Series* No. 50, 1984.

Graner, J. L., *et al*. "William Halsted's cocaine habit." [letter] *Arch Ophthalmol* 102 (December 1984):1746.

Greenberg, R., *et al*. "The role of bound calcium in supersensitivity induced by cocaine." *Br J Pharmacol* 57 (July 1976):329-34.

Grinspoon, L., *et al*. "Coca and cocaine as medicines: a historical review." *J Ethnopharmacol* 3 (March-May 1981):149-59.

Hankes, L. "Cocaine: Today's drug." *J Fla Med Assoc* 71 (April 1984):235-239.

Hanna, J. M., *et al.* "Use of coca leaf in southern Peru: adaptation or addiction." *Bull Narc* 29 (January-March 1977):63-74.

Hawks, R. "Cocaine: the material." *Natl Drug Abuse Res Monogr* 13 (May 1977):47-61.

Helfrich, A. A., *et al.* "A clinical profile of 136 cocaine abusers." *Natl Inst Drug Abuse Res Monogr Ser* 43 (April 1983):343-350.

Henseling, M., *et al.* "The effect of cocaine on the distribution of labelled noradrenaline in rabbit aortic strips and on efflux of radioactivity from the strips." *Naunyn Schmiedebergs Arch Pharmacol* 292 (March 1976):231-41.

Hewer, C. L. "Cocaine and coca." [letter] *Anesthesia* 31 (March 1976):294.

Ho, B. T., *et al.* "Behavioral effects of cocaine-metabolic and neurochemical approach." pp. 229-40. In: Ellinwood, E. H., Jr., and M. M. Kilbey (ed.). *Cocaine and other stimulants*. New York:Plenum Press, 1977.

Howard, R. E., *et al.* "Acute myocardial infarction following cocaine abuse in a young woman with normal coronary arteries." *JAMA* 254 (July 1985):95-96.

Hunt, D. E., *et al.* "An instant shot of 'aah': cocaine use among methadone clients." *J Psychoative Drugs* 16 (July-September 1984):217-227.

Hutchinson, R. R., *et al.* "The effects of cocaine on an aggressive behavior of mice, pigeons and squirrel monkeys." pp. 247-80. In: Ellinwood, E. H., Jr., and M. M. Kilbey (ed.). *Cocaine and other stimulants*. New York: Plenum Press, 1977.

"Images of cocaine." [editorial] *Lancet* 2 (Nov 26, 1983):1231-1232.

Itkonen, J., *et al.* "Pulmonary dysfunction in 'freebase' cocaine users." *Arch Intern Med* 144 (November 1984)):2195-2197.

Javaid, J. I., *et al.* "Cocaine Plasma Concentration: Relations to Physiological and Subjective Effects in Humans." *Science* 220 (October 1978):227-228.

_____ "Determination of cocaine in human urine, plasma and red blood cells by gas-liquid chromatography." *J Chromatogr* 152 (May 1978):105-113.

_____ "Effects of intravenous cocaine on MHPG excretion in man." pp. 665-73. In: Ellinwood, E. H., Jr., and M. M. Kilbey (ed.). *Cocaine and other stimulants*. New York: Plenum Press, 1977.

Jeri, F. R. "Coca-paste smoking in some Latin American countries: a severe and unabated form of addiction." *Bull Narc* (April-June 1984):15-31.

Johns, M. E., *et al*. "Cocaine use by the otolaryngologist: a survey." *Trans Am Acad Ophthalmol Otolaryngol* 84 (November-December 1977):969-973.

Johns, M. E., *et al*. "Metabolism of intranasally applied cocaine." *Ann Otol Rhinol Laryngol* 86 (May-June 1977):342-347.

Jonsson, S., *et al*. "Acute cocaine poisoning. Importance of treating seizures and acidosis." *Am J Med* 75 (December 1983): 1061-1064.

Kegley, C. F., *et al*. "Cocaine: old drug, new problems." *J Sch Health* 47 (December 1977):600-602.

Khantzian, E. J. "An extreme case of cocaine dependence and marked improvement with methylphenidate treatment." *Am J Psychiatry* 140 (June 1983):784-785.

Kilbey, M. M., *et al*. "Chronic administration of stimulant drugs: response modification." pp. 409-29. In: Ellinwood, E. H., Jr., and M. M. Kilbey (ed.). *Cocaine and other stimulants*. New York: Plenum Press, 1977.

_____ "Reverse tolerance to stimulant-induced abnormal behavior." Life Sci 20 (Mar 15, 1977):1063-75.

_____ "The effects of chronic cocaine pretreatment on kindled seizures and behavioral stereotypes." *Exp Neurol* 64 (May 1979):306-314.

Kleber, H. D. and F. H. Gawin. "The spectrum of cocaine abuse and its treatment." *J Clin Psychiatry* 45(12 Pt. 2) (December 1984):18-23.

Kloss, M. W., *et al*. "Cocaine-mediated hepatotoxicity. A critical review." Biochem Pharmacol 33 (January 1984):169-73.

Kossowsky, W. A., and A. F. Lyon. "Cocaine and acute myocardial infarction: A probable connection." *Chest* 86 (November 1984): 729-731.

Kozel, Nicholas J. and Edgar H. Adams (eds.). "Cocaine Use in America: Epidemiologic and Clinical Perspectives." Rockville,

MD: *National Institute on Drug Abuse Research Monograph Series* No. 61, 1985.

Kulberg, A., *et al.* "Who has bugs?" [letter] *Pediatrics* 73 (January 1984):117.

Lesko, L. M., *et al.* "Iatrogenous cocaine psychosis." [letter] *N Engl J Med* 307 (October 28, 1982):1153.

Llewellyn, M. E., *et al.* "Relative reinforcer magnitude under a nonindependent concurrent schedule of cocaine reinforcement in rhesus monkeys." *J Exp Anal Behav* 25 (January 1976): 81-91.

Llosa, T. "Follow-up study of 28 cocaine paste addicts treated by open cingulotomy." Paper presented at the 7th World Congress of Psychiatry, Vienna, 1983.

Mandell, A. J., *et al.* "Neurobiological antagonism of cocaine by lithium." pp. 187-200. In: Ellinwood, E. H., Jr., and M. M. Kilbey (ed.). *Cocaine and other stimulants*. New York: Plenum Press, 1977.

Masters, N. J. "Brompton cocktail." [letter] *Lancet* 2 (Jul 7, 1979): 47.

Matsuzaki, M. "Alteration in pattern of EEG activities and convulsant effect of cocaine following chronic administration in the rhesus monkey." *Electroencephalogr Clin Neurophysiol* 45 (July 1978):1-15.

Matsuzaki, M., *et al.* "Cocaine: tolerance to its convulsant and cardiorespiratory stimulating effects in the monkey." *Life Sci* 19 (July 15, 1976):193-203.

McAuley, J. E. "Carl Koller: the man and the drug." *Br Dent J* 158 (May 1985):339-342.

McKenna, M. L., *et al.* "The role of dopamine in the discriminative stimulus properties of cocaine." *Neuropharmacology* 19 (March 1980):297-303.

McKenna, M., *et al.* "Induced tolerance to the discriminative stimulus properties of cocaine." *Pharmacol Biochem Behav* 7 (September 1977):273-276.

Melzack, R., *et al.* "The Brompton mixture: effects on pain in cancer patients." *Can Med Assoc J* 115 (July 1976):125-129.

Miller, G. W., Jr. "The cocaine habit." *Am Fam Physician* 31 (February 1985):173-176.

Miller, S. M. "Cocaine toxicity." [letter] *JAMA* 239 (June 9, 1978): 2448-2449.

Millman, R. B. "Adverse effects of cocaine." [letter] *Hosp Community Psychiatry* 33 (October 1982):804.

Misra, A. L., *et al*. "Calcium-binding property of cocaine and some of its active metabolites-formation of molecular complexes." *Res Commun Chem Pathol Pharmacol* 11 (August 1975): 663-666.

____ "Disposition and metabolism of [3H] cocaine in acutely and chronically treated monkeys." *Drug Alcohol Depend* 2 (July 1977):261-272.

Misra, A. L., *et al*. "Molecular complexes of cocaine, its active metabolites and some other stimulants with thiamine." *Res Commun Chem Pathol Pharmacol* 15 (October 1976):401-404.

Mittleman, H. S., *et al*. "Cocaine." *Am J Nurs* 84 (September 1984):1092-1095.

Mittleman, R. E., *et al*. "Death caused by recreational cocaine use." *JAMA* 252 (October 12, 1984):1889-1893.

Mount, B. M., *et al*. "Use of the Brompton mixture in treating the chronic pain of malignant disease." *Can Med Assoc J* 115 (July 1976):122-124.

Mule, Joseph S. "The Pharmacodynamics of Cocaine abuse." *Psychiatric Ann* 14 (October, 1984):724-727.

Mule, S. J., *et al*. "Cocaine: distribution and metabolism in animals." pp. 215-28. In: Ellinwood, E. H., Jr., and M. M. Kilbey (ed.). *Cocaine and other stimulants*. New York: Plenum Press, 1977.

Myers, J. A., and M. P. Earnest. "Generalized seizures and cocaine abuse." *Neurology* 34 (May 1984):675-676.

Nakamura, G. R., *et al*. "Fatalities from cocaine overdoses in Los Angeles County." *Clin Toxicol* 18 (August 1981):895-905.

"National surveillance of cocaine use and related health consequences." *MMWR* 31 (May 28, 1982):265-268, 273.

Novick, D. M., *et al*. "Abuse of antibiotics by abusers of parenteral heroin or cocaine." *South Med J* 77 (March 1984):302-303.

Nuckols, Cardwell C. "Cocaine." *The Counselor* (January-February 1984):11-23.

Oei, T. P. "Effects of body weight reduction and food deprivation on cocaine self-administration." *Pharmacol Biochem Behav* 19 (September 1983):453-455.

Olson, K., *et al*. "Management of cocaine poisoning." [letter] *Ann Emerg Med* 12 (October 1983):655-657.

Perez-Reyes, M., *et al*. "Freebase cocaine smoking." *Clinical Pharmacology and Therapeutics* 32 (October 1982):459-465.

Petersen, R. C. "Cocaine: an overview." *Natl Inst Drug Abuse Res Monogr Ser Series* No. 13 (May 1977):5-15.

Petersen, Robert and Richard Stillman (eds.). "Cocaine: 1977." *NIDA Research Monograph* No. 13, (May, 1977).

Pettit, H. O., *et al*. "Destruction of dopamine in the nucleus accumbens selectively attenuates cocaine but not heroin self-administration in rats." Berlin: *Psychopharmacology* 84(2) 1984:167-173.

Post, R. M. "Cocaine psychoses: a continuum model." *Am J Psychiatry* 132 (March 1975):225-231.

Post, R. M., and Kopanda, R. T. "Cocaine, kindling and psychosis." [letter] *Am J Psychiatry* 133 (June 1976):627-634.

Post, R. M., *et al*. "Increasing effects of repetitive cocaine administration in the rat." *Nature* 260 (April 22, 1976):731-732.

_____ "Cocaine, kindling, and reverse tolerance." *Lancet* 1 (February 15, 1975):409-10.

_____ "Progressive effects of cocaine on behavior and central amine metabolism in rhesus monkeys: relationship to kindling and psychosis." *Biol Psychiatry* 11 (August 1976):403-419.

Pradhan, S., *et al*. "Correlation of behavioral and neurochemical effects of acute administration of cocaine in rats." *Life Sci* 22 (May 15, 1978):1737-1743.

Purdie, F. R. "Therapy for pulmonary edema following IV 'freebase' cocaine use." *Ann Emer Med* 11(4) 1982:228-229.

Rappolt, R. T., *et al*. "Propranolol: a specific antagonist to cocaine." *Clin Toxicol* 10(3) 1977:265-71.

Rappolt, R. T., Sr. "Clinical toxicologist's notebook." *Clin Toxicol* 7(5) 1974:541-543.

_____ "Propranolol in the treatment of cardiopressor effect of cocaine." [letter] *N Engl J Med* 295 (Aug 19, 1976):448.

Ravin, J. G., *et al*. "Blindness due to illicit use of topical cocaine." *Ann Ophthalmol* 11 (June 1979):863-864.

Ravitz, A. J., *et al*. "Effects of amphetamine, methyiphenidate and cocaine on serum prolactin concentrations in the male rat." *Life Sci* 21 (July 15, 1977):267-72.

Resnick, R. B., and E. B. Resnick. "Cocaine abuse and its treatment." *Psychiatr Clin North Am* 7 (December 1984): 713-728.

Ritchie, J., *et al*. "Cocaine, Procaine and Other Synthetic Local Anesthetics." pp. 379-382. In: Goodman and Gilman. *The Pharmacologic Basis of Therapeutics*. New York: Macmillan, 1970.

Rosecan, J. "The treatment of cocaine abuse with imipramine, L-tyrosine, and L-tryptophan." Paper presented at the 7th World Congress of Psychiatry, Vienna, Austria, July 14, 1983.

Schachne, J. S., *et al*. "Coronary-artery spasm and myocardial infarction associated with cocaine use." [letter] *N Engl J Med* 310 (June 21, 1984):1665-1666.

Schell-Kruger, J., *et al*. "Cocaine: discussion on the role of dopamine in the biochemical mechanism of action." pp. 273-407. In: Ellinwood, E. H., Jr., and M. M. Kilbey (ed.). *Cocaine and other stimulants*. New York: Plenum Pres, 1977.

Schenck, N. L. "Cocaine: its use and misuse in otolaryngology." *Trans Am Acad Ophthalmol Otolaryngol* 80 (July-August 1975):343-351.

Schenck, N. L. "The case for cocaine." *Med Times* 104 (February 1976):80-82, 85.

Schnoll, S. "Cocaine." [letter] *JAMA* 232 (May 19, 1975):706.

Sears, B. E. "Potential hazards of the medical administration of cocaine." *J Okla State Med Assoc* 73 (April 1980):97-100.

Shuster, L., *et al*. "Liver damage from cocaine in mice." *Life Sci* 20 (March 15, 1977):1035-1041.

Siegal, R. K. "Cocaine and Sexual Dysfunction: The Curse of Mama Coca." *J Psychoactive Drugs* 14 (January-June 1982): 71-74.

____ "Cocaine and the privileged class: a review of historical and contemporary images." *Adv Alcohol Subst Abuse Winter* 4(2) 1984:37-49.

____ "Cocaine aroma in the treatment of cocaine dependency." [letter] *J Clin Psychopharmacol* 4 (February 1984):61-62.

____ "Cocaine hallucinations." *Am J Psychiatry* 135 (March 1978): 309-314.

____ "Cocaine: recreational use and intoxication." *N Inst Drug Abuse Res Monogr Ser Series* 13 (May 1977):119-136.

____ "Cocaine smoking." *J Psychoactive Drugs* 14 (October-December 1982):271-359.

____ "Cocaine substitutes." [letter] *N Engl J Med* 302 (April 3, 1980):817-818.

____ "Moreno and the first study on cocaine: a historical note and translation." *J Psychoactive Drugs* 15 (July-September 1983): 219-220.

____ "Treatment of cocaine abuse: historical and contemporary perspectives." *J Psychoactive Drugs* 17 (January-March 1985): 1-9.

Siguel, E. "Characteristics of clients admitted to treatment for cocaine abuse." *Natl Inst Drug Abuse Res Monogr Ser Series* 13 (May 1977):201-210.

Small, G. W., *et al*. "Trazodone and cocaine abuse." [letter] *Arch Gen Psychiatry* 42 (May 1985):524.

Smart, R. G., *et al*. "Cocaine use among adults and students." *Can J Public Health* 72 (November-December 1981):433-438.

Smith, A. C., *et al*. "Ethanol enhancement of cocaine-induced hepatotoxicity." *Biochem Pharmacol* 30 (March 1, 1981): 453-458.

Snyder, R. D., *et al*. "Intranasal cocaine abuse in an allergists office." *Ann Allergy* 54 (June 1985):489-492.

Staats, G. R., *et al*. "Changing orientations among cocaine users: consequences of involvement in community distribution networks." *Am J Drug Alcohol Abuse* 6(3) 1979:283-290.

____ "Regulatory factors affecting cocaine use in a rural area." *Br J Addict* 74 (December 1979):391-402.

Stamler, R. T., *et al*. "Illicit traffic and abuse of cocaine." *Bull Narc* 36 (April-June 1984):45-55.

Stark, T. W., *et al*. "Cocaine toxicity." *Ear Nose Throat J* 62 (March 1983):155-158.

Stretch, R. "Discrete-trial control of cocaine self-injection behavior in squirrel monkeys: effects of morphine, naloxone, and chlorpromazine." *Can J Physiol Pharmacol* 55 (August 1977): 778-790.

Stretch, R., *et al.* "Cocaine self-injection behaviour under schedules of delayed reinforcement in monkeys." *Can J Physiol Pharmacol* 54 (August 1976):632-638.

Stripling, J. S., *et al.* "Augmentation of the behavioral and electrophysiologic response to cocaine by chronic administration in the rat." *Exp Neurol* 54 (March 1977):546-564.

Tennant, F. S., Jr. "Effect of cocaine dependence on plasma phenylalanine and tyrosine levels and on urinary MHPG excretion." *Am J Psychiatry* 142 (October 1985):1200-1201.

Tennant, F. S., Jr., *et al.* "Cocaine and amphetamine dependence treated with desipramine." *Natl Inst Drug Abuse Res Monogr Ser* 43 (April 1983):351-355.

Twycross, R. "Value of cocaine in opiate-containing elixirs." [letter] *Br Med J* 2 (November 19, 1977):1348.

Valente, D., *et al.* "Hair as the sample in assessing morphine and cocaine addiction" [letter] *Clin Chem* 27 (November 1981): 1952-1953.

Van Dyke, C. and R. Byck. "Cocaine: 1884-1974." pp. 1-30. In: Ellinwood, E. H., Jr., and M. M. Kilbey (ed.). *Cocaine and other stimulants*. New York: Plenum Press, 1977.

Van Dyke, C., *et al.* "Cocaine and lidocaine have similar psychological effects after intranasal application." *Life Sci* 24 (January 15, 1979):271-274.

_____ "Cocaine." *Sci Am* 246 (March, 1982):128-141.

_____ "Oral cocaine: plasma concentrations and central effects." *Science* 200 (April 14, 1978):211-213.

Vilensky, W. "Illicit and licit drugs causing perforation of the nasal septum." *J Forensic Sci* 27 (October 1982):958-962.

Washton, A. M., *et al.* "Adolescent cocaine abusers." [letter] *Lancet* 2 (September 29, 1984):746.

_____ "Intranasal cocaine addiction." [letter] *Lancet* 2 (December 10, 1983):1374.

_____ "Opiate and cocaine dependents. Techniques to help counter the rising tide." *Postgrad Med* 77 (April 1985):293-297, 300.

Webster, Terry. *Needing Cocaine*. Center City: Hazelden, 1985.

Weiss, R. D., *et al*. "Treatment of chronic cocaine abuse and attention deficit disorder, residual type, with magnesium pemoline." *Drug Alcohol Depend* 15 (May 1985):69-72.

Wesson, D. R., *et al*. "Cocaine: its use for central nervous system stimulation including recreational and medical uses." *Natl Inst Drug Abuse Res Monogr Ser Series* 13 (May 1977):137-152.

Welti, C. V., *et al*. "Death caused by recreational cocaine use." *JAMA* 241 (June 3, 1979):2519-2522.

Wilson, M. C. "The effect of cocaine and D-amphetamine on punished responding." *Arch Int Pharmacodyn Ther* 227 (May 1977):98-105.

Wilson, M. C., *et al*. "Intravenous cocaine lethality in the rat." *Pharmacol Res Commun* 10 (March 1978):243-256.

Woolverton, W. L., *et al*. "Tolerance and cross-tolerance to cocaine and d-amphetamine." *J Pharmacol Exp Ther* 205 (June 1978):525-535.

Books

Adler, Patricia A. *Wheeling and Dealing: An Ethnography of an Upper-Level Drug Dealing and Smuggling Community*. New York: Columbia University Press, 1985.

American Psychiatric Association. *Diagnostic and Statistical Manual III (DSM III)*. Washington, DC: American Psychiatric Association, 1980.

Anglin, Lise. *Cocaine: A Selection of Annotated Papers from 1880 to 1984 Concerning Health Effects*. Toronto: Addiction Research Foundation, 1985.

Ashley, Richard. *Cocaine: Its History, Uses and Effects*. New York: Warner Books, 1975.

Baum, Joanne. *One Step Over the Line*. San Francisco: Harper and Row Publishers, 1985.

Beckhard, Arthur J., and William D. Crane. *Cancer, Cocaine and Courage; The Story of Dr. William Halsted*. New York: Julio Messner, Inc., 1900.

Brecher, E. *Licit and Illicit Drugs: The Consumers Union Report on Narcotics, Stimulants, Inhalants, Hallucinogens and*

Marijuana, Including Caffeine, Nicotine and Alcohol. New York: Little, Brown, 1972.

Brink, Carla J. (ed.). *Cocaine: A Symposium*. Madison: Wisconsin Institute on Drug Abuse, 1985.

Byck, Robert (ed.). *Cocaine Papers*. New York: Stonehill Publishing Company, 1974.

Cocaine Papers: From Freud to Freebase. rev. ed. Phoenix, AZ: Do It Now Foundation, 1986.

Cohen, Sidney. *Cocaine: The Bottom Line*. Washington, DC: American Council on Drug Education, 1985.

Ellinwood, Everett H. "Amphetamines and stimulus drugs." In: *Drug Use in America; Problem in Perspective*. Vol. 1, National Commission on Marijuana and Drug Abuse. Washington, DC: GPO, 1973.

Emboden, William A., Jr. *Narcotic Plants*. New York: Macmillan, 1972.

Englemann, Jeanne M. *Cocaine: Beyond the Looking Glass Discussion Guide*. Center City: Hazelden, 1984.

Erickson, Patricia, G. *The Steel Drug: Cocaine in Perspective.* Lexington, MA: Lexington Books, 1987.

Gold, Mark S., M. D. *800-Cocaine*. New York: Bantam Books, 1984.

Goldman, Bob. *Death in the Locker Room*. Tucson, AZ: The Body Press, 1987.

Grinspoon, L. and J. Bakalar. *Cocaine: A Drug and Its Social Evolution*. New York: Basic Books, 1976.

Hafen, Brent Q. and Kathryn J. Frandsen. *Cocaine*. Center City, MN: Hazelden, 1982.

Hyde, Margaret O. *Addictions*. New York: McGraw-Hill, 1978.

Johanson, Chris-Ellyn. *Cocaine: A New Epidemic*. Edgemont, PA: Chelsea House, 1986.

Kahn, E. J. The Big Drink: The Story of Coca-Cola. New York: Random House, 1960.

Kennedy, Joseph. *Coca Exotica: The Illustrated Story of Cocaine*. New York: Cornwall Books, 1985.

Keys, T. E. *The History of Surgical Anesthesia*. New York: Dover, 1963.

Learn About Cocaine. Center City, MN: Hazelden, 1983.

Lee, D. *Cocaine Handbook: An Essential Reference*. Berkeley: And/Or Press, 1981.

Long, Robert Emmet, ed. *Drugs and American Society*. New York: Wilson, 1985.

McInerney, Jay. *Bright Lights, Big City*. New York: Vintage Contemporaries, 1984.

Mariani, Angelo. *Coca and Its Therapeutic Application*. 2d ed. New York: J. N. Jaros, 1892.

Meyers, Annie C. *Eight Years in Cocaine Hell*. Chicago: St. Luke Society Press, 1902.

Mills, James. *The Underground Empire: Where Crime and Governments Embrace*. Garden City, NY: Doubleday, 1986.

Milsra, A. L. and S. J. Mule (ed.). *Cocaine: Chemical, Biological, Clinical, Social, and Treatment Aspects*. Cleveland: CRC Press, 1976.

Mortimer, W. G. *Peru History of Coca, The Divine Plant of The Incas, With an Introductory Account of the Incas and of the Andean Indians of Today*. New York: J. H. Vail & Co., 1901.

Moser, Brian. *The Cocaine Eaters*. New York: Taplinger, 1967.

Musto, David F. *The American Disease: Origins of Narcotic Control*. New Haven and London: Yale Univ Press, 1973.

National Clearinghouse for Drug Abuse Information. *Cocaine*. Report Series 11, No. 1. Washington, DC: GPO, 1971.

Nuckols, Cardwell, C. *Cocaine: From Dependency to Recovery*. Bradenton, FL: Human Services Institute, Inc., 1987.

O'Connell, Kathleen R. *End of the Line: Quitting Cocaine*. Philadelphia: Westminster, 1985.

Petersen, D. Majken (ed.). *Cocaine: Crisis in Our Land*. Tallahassee, FL: Florida Alcohol and Drug Abuse Association, 1986.

Phillips, Joel, and R. D. Wynne. *Cocaine: The Mystique and the Reality*. New York: Avon Books, 1980.

Plasket, Bruce J., and Ed Quillen. *The White Stuff*. New York: Dell, 1985.

Ray, D. S. *Drugs, Society and Behavior*. St. Louis: C.V. Mosby, 1972.

Rozel, Nicholas J., and E. H. Adams. *Cocaine Use in America: Epidemiological and Clinical Perspectives*. National Institute on Drug Abuse Monograph No. 61. Washington, DC: GPO, 1985.

Sabbag, Robert. *Snow Blind*. New York: Avon Books, 1976.

Senay, Edward C. *Substance Abuse Disorders in Clinical Practice*. Boston: John Wright, 1983.

Smart, Richard. *The Snow Papers: A Memoir of Illusion, Power-Lust and Cocaine*. (ed. J. Johnson). Boston: Atlantic Monthly, 1985.

Sparkman, J.C., Jr. *The Cocaine Handbook*. Jacksonville Beach, FL: Creative Alternatives Press, 1985.

Spotts, James V., and Franklin C. Shontz. *Cocaine Users: A Representative Case Approach*. New York: Free Press, 1980.

Stone, Nannette, *et al. Cocaine: Seduction and Solution*. New York: Clarkson N. Potter, Inc., 1984.

Stone, Robert. *Children of Light*. New York: Alfred A. Knopf, Inc., 1986.

Sutphen, Trenna. *Final Cut: A Life Changing Self-Help Program t Quit Cocaine*. Malibu, CA: Trenna Productions, 1984.

Treatii the Cocaine Abuser. Center City: Hazelden, 1985.

Washton, Arnold M. and Mark S. Gold (ed.). *Cocaine: A Clinician's Handbook*. New York: The Gulford Press, 1987.

Watson, John H. (ed. Nicholas Meyer). *The Seven Per-Cent Solution*. New York: Ballantine Books, 1974.

Webster, Terry. *Needing Cocaine*. Center City, MN: Hazelden, 1985.

Weil, Andrew. *Chocolate to Morphine*. Boston: Houghton Mifflin, 1983.

_____ *The Natural Mind*. Boston: Houghton Mifflin, 1972.

Weiner, Michael A. *Getting Off Cocaine; 30 Days to Freedom: The Step-By-Step Program of Nutrition and Exercise*. New York: Avon, 1984.

Weiss, Roger D. and Steven M. Mirin. *Cocaine*. American Psychiatric Press, Inc., 1987.

Wilford, B. *Drug Abuse: A Guide For The Primary Care Physician*. Chicago: AMA, 1981.

Wisotsky, Stephen. *Breaking the Impasse in the War on Drugs*. New York: Greenwood Press, 1986.

Woodley, Richard. *Dealer: Portrait of A Cocaine Merchant*. New York: Holt, Rinehart & Winston, 1971.

Wynn Associates. *Cocaine: Summaries of Psychosocial Research*. Rockville, MD: National Institute on Drug Abuse, 1977.

Zinberg, Norman E. *Drug Set and Setting*. New Haven: Yale University Press, 1984.

INDEX